#4 Hatch

An Autobiography

Jack Stamper

#4 Hatch

Front cover photograph: Crew members of the Albemarle, taken in Havana, Cuba, 1954

First published 2010 by Countyvise Limited,
14 Appin Road, Birkenhead, CH41 9HH

Copyright © 2010 Jack Stamper

The right of Jack Stamper to be identified as the author of this work has been asserted by him in accordance with the Copyright, Design and Patents Act 1988.

British Library Cataloguing in Publication Data.
A catalogue record for this book is available from the British Library.

ISBN 978 1 906823 40 5

All rights reserved. No part of this publication may be reproduced, stored in a retrieval system, or transmitted, in any other form, or by any other means, electronic, chemical, mechanic, photograph copying, recording or otherwise, without the prior permission of the publisher.

Foreword

I dedicate this story to my wife Eileen, and to my daughters Jacqueline, Michelle, my sons Gerard and Paul, also Sue Steel and Dave Berry. Without them it would not be a story. I know I have been a pain in asking for their help as I am still a dinosaur regarding the computer, but it has been fun writing it.

This title has been with me for over twenty years. Why # 4 HATCH? This came about because freighters that had been built in the fifties and before, had five hatches, three forward of the bridge, and two aft of the bridge. The fourth hatch was nearest to the accommodation, there being no recreation room. The normal recreation was taken after the evening meal and having had a shower. Those of the crew on day-work with their beer ration in a cold water bucket would sit on the hatch cover and put the world to rights.

#4 Hatch

Jack Stamper

Contents

CHAPTER		PAGE
1	The Hungry Thirties	1
2	Tough Times in my Childhood	4
3	Street Games	15
4	The Best Game - Football	18
5	The Travelling Salesman	24
6	Going to the Pictures	28
7	Great Adventures	32
8	Brunswick Gardens	35
9	Just Before the War	40
10	Camping Money	45
11	My First Job	48
12	The War Years	53
13	The Apprentice Years	60
14	Liverpool O. H. Railway	63
15	Dock Road, Our Playground	66
16	Young Lad's Games	73
17	My Life on the Docks	79
18	Humour on the Docks	93
19	The Army Years	96
20	A Near Disaster	107
21	Some Amazing Stories	120
22	Swallowing the Anchor	122
23	Our European Tour	128
24	My Grandma	131
25	Ship's Carpenter	135
26	Married to Eileen	149
27	Politics	155
28	I Became a Joiner	158
29	Working on the Teaching Hospital	165
30	Shrewsbury Trials	167

31	Family life	174
32	Knowsley council	178
33	Political landscapes change	182
34	My children and family today	185
35	Liverpool then and now	194
36	Finally retirement	202

CHAPTER ONE

The Hungry Thirties

I hope that by writing my autobiography it will encourage other people to write their own story. I believe everybody has a story to tell.

My story reaches back 80 years so I hope you will travel with me and find some enjoyment in reading of the ups and downs of my life.

My story began in the early Thirties. I was born 2nd March 1930 at number 67 Byles Street in the Dingle area of Toxteth, Liverpool, England. My brother Eddy was the first born in 1928.

These times were known as the "Hungry Thirties". The house we lived in was originally my grandparent's house, until they moved up market to Dombey Street and then my parents moved into the Byles Street house. The house consisted of two bedrooms and was gas lit with a flagged floor. The stairs to the bedroom were near the front door and there was Lino on the stairs, no hallway. The sink was in the tiny yard and our only means of heating was the coal fire which is where we boiled the water by kettle.

I remember my mother putting the meat in the oven which was heated by the fire. I can still smell the aroma. All in all it was better than living in the courts at the bottom of our street.

The years of "Means Testing" meant that if you had the luxury of a wireless (radio) or a gramophone or any other valuable you were told to sell it off and the money you got for it was for you to live on. This was Toryism at its worst. This was also a time for the "haves and have-nots" as it always was.

Stanley Baldwin was the Prime Minister. This was the man who owned Baldwin Steel of South Wales; the company that made a profit by selling steel to Germany in the thirties that was used to build their armaments to fight Britain.

My parents were very young when they got married in 1928. My father was only seventeen and my mother was nineteen. I was two years old when my mother left home, to work in the Isle of Man. It was a seasonal job, from April to the end of September.

After just a couple of years the marriage was beginning to show cracks. The possible reason being that she may have come from the 'wrong side of the tracks' as in those days even among the working class there was a stigma attached to being a labourer. It was called 'looking down your nose'. If you had some ladders and paintbrushes then that would put you a class above the labourer because that was considered having your own business. This is how this society thought in the earlier part of the century. My grandfather on my father's side had a painters and decorators business but on my mother's side they were dock labourers. This would be at the bottom of the ladder, and unfortunately that's the way people thought.

I remember the times when my father would take Eddy and me to the Pier Head landing stage to meet my mother off the Isle of Man boat. This event happened at the end of the holiday season in September as she left home in the May time and returned in September.

The love they had between them had been short lived. It got to such an extent that my mother reported my father to the dole office for 'working on the side'. He probably did and pocketed the money and was duly given a month in gaol.

Times were very hard during those years. As my mother had found work in the Isle of Man for a period of 16 weeks it was left to my father to manage the money which my mother had sent home.

He got me a place at St. Paul's school when I was only three and a half years of age; the normal age for starting school was five years of age. Both Eddy and I attended St Paul's. I can vaguely remember my first day at school but the thing I recall vividly is that I wore a big woollen scarf tied crossways, with a big safety pin at the back.

I remember during the winter period the bottles of milk were placed along the hot pipes. These were one third pint bottles with a wide neck and a round cardboard stopper, in which you punched a small hole to put in your straw. These were given out at mid-morning. I think they were a penny per bottle. I also remember some classes had a big fire in the grate.

The first level classes were known as the babies or infants classes. Like the girls we had to wear the same smocks.

As pictured, find me on the photograph. I am on the 2nd row, 1st left, my hair black as coal, with pudding face. Note the faces on the children. The caption could read "What is that man doing under that black cape"? He was taking our photograph. At that age, you couldn't care less what you were wearing. I believe this age is where friendships first began.

St Paul's Infants School – 1933
I'm first lad on the left of centre row, aged 3

CHAPTER TWO

Tough Times in my Childhood

The street was always full of kids. My mate was Ronnie Ross and he lived in Back Whitfield Street. Next door to us was the Green family. They were a big family. Mr. Green had had both of his legs blown off in the Great War. He used to sit outside on the pavement and we could see his tin legs. I remember during the elections, he would vote for the Tories. I don't know why!

After the First World War the slogan was to build decent houses and get rid of the slums. But the government of the day was a Liberal government headed by Lloyd George. "Houses will be built for heroes," was their pledge to the poor buggers coming home from "Hell" in France. But they came back to the shit holes they left behind. The houses where we lived, were up for demolition before the First World War. I believe our house was built in the 1850s. People lived in squalor for another 20 years after the First World War. There were 3 million on the dole. There were children who ran barefoot through the streets, even in the thirties.

There was an organization called the "Police Welfare Fund" who gave out clothes to the needy but my mother thought it was undignified to accept charity from these Welfare funds. This meant my brother and I were more fortunate than others as we always had good shoes from the English Leather Shop on Bold Street.

I remember Bold Street. In the thirties this street was the poshest street in the north of England. It could equal Bond Street in London. The road surface was made of hardwood blocks so the carts would not make a noise. In the nineteenth century Bold Street was for the well-to-do people. It is known that the shipwrights' wives travelled in handsome cabs to call to the grocers to buy their butter. They tasted it on a gold sovereign piece.

In those days shipwrights were the top trade. Where did it all go wrong? I was a shipwright! My wife got margarine. They had some fine shops in Bold Street, such as Waring & Gillows, the top furniture shop in the country, Swears & Wells which sold fur coats and Cripps the gown shop. The shop on the corner of Newington and Bold Street sold Rolls Royce cars; it was the finest shopping street in the north....

Saturday night was bath night. My mam got the tin bath out of the yard and it was put in front of the fire, the kettle on the hob. I had to get in second after Eddy using the same bath water. We would get dried in front of the fire. We only had gas back then, no electricity. We would listen to the wireless at night. Some of our favourite programmes were 'In Town Tonight', 'Band Wagon with Arthur Askey' and Radio Luxemburg, which was a new station on the wireless.

In the winter we would take out the oven shelves and wrapping them in paper put them under the blankets to warm the bed up. Next morning if you put your feet on the iron shelves they would be freezing cold.

On Sunday mornings my mother made porridge from the oats that had been soaked overnight. We had codfish, we called "salt-dolly" and we would spread margarine over the salt fish.

The world was a harsher place back then with three million on the dole.

My father was unemployed for eight years. He, like many, got 'work on the side' called "moonlighting". "The Unemployment Assistance Board" commonly known as the Parish was a scheme supposed to alleviate the poor. "My arse," as Ricky Tomlinson would say. The building is still there today.

In High Park Street you would have to present yourself to the officer behind the desk. Questions were asked. Have you any possessions to sell - a gramophone or the treasured radio? The parish was heartless and soulless; they would let you live on the street if they could.

I remember once my mother took my brother and me up to the parish to ask for some money to live on, but the parish turned her down. My mother screamed back at the officer saying that, "if the 'bloody kids' were scruffy with snots tripping us up we would have got a better response".

Once a week, the Salvation Army would bring the 'Soup wagon' around the streets. They would ring a hand bell shouting, "Pea soup!" and people would rush out with their basins and pans, anything to carry the soup home. My mother would give us the belt for getting it as she thought it below her dignity to accept the charity of free soup. We still brought it in anyway, and it was great. Even she had to admit she did enjoy it.

At the bottom of our street there were two courts. There was a shared tap stand in the centre of the court. There were also a couple of communal toilets shared between the eight houses, four on each side of the court. There was one bin shared between the eight houses. All the houses were dark and dingy. That was what it was like to live in abject poverty and Liverpool had plenty of areas like this, mainly to the north of the city.

Streets were badly lit in those days. I remember the lamp-lighter. He would come round with the long pole to turn the gaslights on. The same man would have the job of cleaning the glass in the lamps as he had a small ladder for this purpose. Later on they put time switches in the lamps. They were never vandalized, as these lights were essential. The only roads that were lit by electricity were the main roads.

I remember that some poor kids had no shoes to wear and had to run barefoot. Life expectancy for men was fifty-five to sixty and women a few years longer. There was a high infant mortality rate during this period. Diseases such as rickets, dysentery, and consumption (TB) were endemic.

The old houses were bug-ridden with cockroaches, rats and mice. If there was chicken pox in your neighbours' houses and if your own children had not had the disease, it was normal to let your kids play with the children who had chicken pox so that they caught it. This meant it would be over and done with and your children would get over it quickly.

If poor people had a very young baby who had died but they couldn't afford a proper funeral it was known that they would have to get on a tram and take the tiny coffin up to cemetery to bury it. That's what I call real poverty.

The war ended in 1945 and there was a general election soon after. Winston Churchill had been the war time leader of a coalition government but the people remembered the pre-war years under a Conservative government and they returned a Labour government with a handsome majority. The leader of the Labour party was Clem Atlee.

At that time the Labour government brought about Nationalisation. It came about in a big way with coal mines, railways, steel and most importantly the birth of the N.H.S in 1947. It was and is still the envy of the world even though it is very expensive to run.

Before 1947 you had to pay for medical care, as there was no N.H.S. Nye Bevan was the Minister of Health in the Attlee government. Unfortunately there were those who bled the N.H.S.

At first, you could get items such as spectacles and false teeth for free but later on the Labour government brought in prescription charges.

Nye Bevan was very angry at this suggestion and he resigned from his post. Nye was an old fashioned socialist and believed in the principle 'Free for one, free for all'. I think the problem was that the people thought that the N.H.S. was a bottomless pit. People applied for free spectacles, false teeth, hearing aids and other items whether they were needed them or not. It was due to a combination of stupidity, ignorance and greed and I think that prescription charges were inevitable.

As an infant, I suffered from asthma. My mother would have to pay 2/6 a time for me to be treated at the Royal Southern Hospital which was situated in Caryl Street on the corner of Hill Street. I attended twice a week for nine years and 2/6 was a lot of money in those days, the treatment was sun-ray and massages.

During the war, the Royal Southern Hospital was taken over by the Royal Navy, as a barracks. It was called the 'H.M.S. Wellesley'. The sailors used to parade every morning up and down Caryl Street. The leather-gaited Commanding Officer received the salute standing on his dais with his ugly bull terrier alongside him.

Healthwise, these were certainly not the good old days and today's living standards are much better. People are healthier and food is more plentiful today.

However, food both before and during the war was all organic. There were no chemicals or pesticides. A carrot might have looked dirty, with soil but after it was washed it tasted much better than today's carrots. Bread during the war had no whitener or artificial aids. It was a darker colour but it too was much tastier. Unlike today you didn't see many fat people during the war years. I don't think it was due to starvation as we had enough food, despite rationing. I am convinced that since we had to put up with the rationing, we may have been a healthier nation?

In today's society people eat too much. I am also convinced that if people ate one meal a day, yes the world would be a healthier place. The biggest killer today is obesity and I admit I am a bit overweight myself! It is also wrong, when there are still people starving in some other parts of the world. Surely there is enough food in this world to feed everybody and no one needs to starve.

I would say that during the thirties people were more caring, giving and honest. Maybe this was because we were all in the same boat. We all had nothing. You could leave your door open and nobody would steal from you as no-one had anything to steal.

Since my father was on the dole, my mother decided to find work in the Isle of Man as I have already mentioned. She was a very good chef. She got work as the head cook at the Friendship Hotel on Loch Promenade. In Douglas the summer tourist season started in April and ran until the end of September. This left my dad to look after us which must have been quite daunting for him as we were so young at the time.

By this time my brother Eddy was coming up to five years old and I was three and a half. We both started school together.

In those days, the seasons seemed to come at the right times and you could predict the weather for any given month. The winters were bitter but as the spring came it got warmer and this seemed to last for ever. I remember in the summer of 1934 my dad took us both down town on the tram to see King George V and Queen Mary open the Mersey Tunnel. The town was packed with people from far and wide. The wind made the flags flap in the breeze; it seemed everybody was enjoying themselves.

Since my dad was on the dole and our only income was the dole money and money my mother sent from the Isle of Man, my dad made our toys. He was very adept at working with tools and I remember once he made us a fine fort. To make it more realistic he covered the fort with glue and poured sand over it. The rough finish looked great and we also played with our lead soldiers.

We were lucky to be the only grandchildren on my dad's side of the family. Every Christmas, we would go up to grandma's and have our Christmas dinner and our presents. We also went there every Sunday throughout the year. Near Christmas, we would go to the grotto at Lewis' or Blackler's to see Father Christmas. We'd be given a tanner toy, which only ever lasted five minutes before it broke. However, I've seen on the T.V. programme 'Floggit' that today, these toys are worth a lot of money.

Grandfather Stamper 1921

I remember when the old trams. Numbers 1, 3 and 20 came up Park Road near where we lived. The number 1 went from the Pier Head to Garston; the 3 went from the Dingle to Spellow Lane Walton, the 20 from Aigburth to Aintree. Then there was the 'Millie Dasher', or number 45, and also the 21 trams on the Mill Street run.

The tram terminus for the numbers 21 and 45 was at Park Hill Road as Beloe Street was too narrow to allow two trams to pass each other so the trams had to return back along Mill

Street. Later on in 1938 they put in a single line down Beloe Street to join up with the other trams at the junction of Park Road. They would then carry on towards Aigburth and then on to Garston.

As the trams went along Aigburth Road towards Garston there was a section from Aigburth Vale to St Mary's Road that was tree-lined. Some of the branches brushed the sides of the trams.

The trams were cheap to travel on. When it was school holidays, kids could get four rides for a penny but the cheap fare ended at 4pm. In my day, some trams had open fronts and backs and on the top-deck there was a round cage for protection. In the winter the poor tram driver would have a big, red face and a big dewdrop on the end of his nose. He had no protection from the elements except for a hat, cape and a long pair of gloves. It was not a good job especially in the wintertime! Towards the end of the thirties, they modernized the trams.

The tram conductors were a fine set of men. They would help the women up onto the tram, as the tram had two steps, nothing was too much trouble for them. They would put the washing, or a baby's pram, up next to the driver. There was no electric bell push to get the old trams to stop. Instead, there was a long leather strap, which ran from one end of the tram to the other on the ceiling. He would shout, "Hold tight!" as he made one tug to stop, and two tugs on the strap, this would tell the driver to go.

When I was an apprentice, I worked with a shipwright who had been a tram driver in the thirties. He told us about one winter, when the weather was particularly severe. Since the tram had an open-front he decided to get behind the stairs for shelter. Mind you, the tram was moving along the track, he was spotted by the inspector, reported and duly given the sack.

There was one place near us where we went in the summer time. This was the cassey (cast iron river shore) which originated from an area for making iron. Situated at the end of Buckland Street was "St Michael's in the Hamlet", which was constructed of iron; this road led you to the shore. There were steps down to a very narrow strip of sand, adjacent to the pier off Dingle oil jetty. If you were brave enough to venture into the River Mersey, you had to stumble over rocks in thick, oily mud. There was an oil jetty pier, jutting out into the river, where oil tankers discharged their cargo of oil.

At the bottom of the steps, a high sandstone wall, ran along the shore towards Otterspool. Half-way along this wall, there were two very old wooden doors, which history tells us is where the fishermen used as a cold storage for the fish, and at the end of this wall the shore became wider. Starting from the steps there were huge, sandstone blocks about 8ft x 4 x 3ft high and we had great fun jumping from one stone to another.

We took a bottle of water and some sandwiches, and really enjoyed ourselves all day. I don't think the Health and Safety people would allow us to go on the cassey today, as it had a sewerage outlet at high tide.

At the Otterspool end, at the top of the cliffs, there was a nine-hole golf course. They closed it down during the war, and dug huge round holes, in which to place big oil tanks. The tops of the tanks were at ground level and would be camouflaged against enemy aircraft.

In 1984 the area was opened as the International Garden Festival, but some years later it closed. Today, the whole area has been transformed into a private property development. Riverside Drive runs through from Otterspool to the Herculaneum area. The council is building more houses in the International Garden site, but some of the garden site is being retained.

Up to the early part of the 20th century, Otterspool was a small fishing port. There was a little inlet that we called the Lost Dock. There also was a farm known as Jericho Farm, which still keeps its name today. The farm had gone in the thirties.

Jack Stamper

In the 1960s, they finally completed the lovely promenade, which starts at Mersey Road and ends at the Herculaneum riverfront. Most of the foundations were built from material taken from the King's Mersey Tunnel excavations.

At the top of Woodlands Road, there was the "Mossley Hill Zoo". It was a nice little zoo; they had elephants and lots of the usual wildlife. They had a chimpanzee called Mickey. He would throw case balls. I remember a time when a man was taking a photograph of him. He stood about 30 feet away. Mickey threw a ball that smacked him in the face, breaking the camera into several pieces. Mickey thought that was great. Some time later, Mickey broke out of the zoo and made his way to a school near by. I think it was Underlea School. Unfortunately, Mickey was considered a danger to the public, and a police marksman was called to the school. By that time, Mickey was on the roof. He had to be shot and he fell into the schoolyard, dead. When the war came, "Mossley Hill Zoo" had to close. All the animals were donated to a more established Zoo in Chester.

It was a grand sight to see Sefton Park Lake which had rowing boats and small motorboats for hire. People used to sail their model yachts on the lake. Near the rowing boat jetty there was a fine model boat store. This building was a wooden structure with a beautiful design, but alas it was vandalized and burnt down. Recently the council have restored the boat house, but it doesn't have the character of the old boat house. During the wintertime, everybody went skating on the frozen lake. The lake would be frozen solid, which made it quite safe. This was a fine sight to see, as lots of people skated in a chain across the ice.

At that time, there were plenty of park keepers to keep people under control. Near by was an aviary, which had some beautiful birds on show. There were lots of little streams in the park with clear water, not stagnant, as it is now. Near to the aviary, in the small river, was the 'Jolly Roger', a scaled down model ship, which was built in 1922 by an old shipwright whom I worked with, named Alf Acton. He was one of the best boat-builders in Liverpool.

Between the large café and the boat lake, on a small island, was a bandstand. The bands would play there in the summer months; also near the café was the beautiful statue of Eros, which recently has been refurbished, and adjacent to the aviary there was also the statue of Peter Pan.

These were the civilized times of yesterday.

Sefton Park is still the largest public park in the North West. I am glad to hear that the government are giving the council a grant, to bring the park back to life. There are still beautiful Georgian and Victorian houses around the perimeter of the park. The Victorians also built the jockey sands, on which the toffs rode their horses.

These large houses still stand there today, a reminder of those who lived in the houses, who donated the lands to build Sefton Park. Parks are the lungs of the citizens.

CHAPTER THREE

Street Games

As children, we played a variety of games in the street. One game was called Ollys. The rules for Ollys were you had a stone Olly each; we would have to dig three holes 3 x 3in deep in the street, one in the gutter, one in the centre of the street, and one in the opposite gutter. We played in Back Whitfield street, as part of the street was tarmacked and all the other streets were granite sets. Often our mothers would ask, where has the "bloody Olly gone out of the kettle". The main use for the Olly was to keep the inside of the kettle lime free, but we thought we had a better use, for our game.

This game was also played by adults in Princes Park, but with steel cups as holes. The Olly pitch was adjacent to the park lake, or near the bowling green. There was a little green hut, were they would lend you bats and balls. We played on the adjacent field.

To start the game, the first player would attempt to try and get your Olly into the centre hole. If not successful, the following player would try to hit off your Olly. If it were a hit, that player would have another turn, and attempt to put his Olly in the centre hole. After holing out, he would move to the gutter hole, and so on, until you returned back to the centre, then on to the hole at the opposite gutter (you would have potted your Olly four times, to have won). There was a special way of holding the Olly, you would have your thumb at the back, and you would use your two forefingers at the front of the Olly, this would, when delivered, have backspin, and would stop the Olly going foreward. We would play for hours, till we got shouted in for bedtime. This game could be reintroduced to present day children.

I think kids were more energetic in those days. There were many other games to be played such as Heavy On. The unfortunate one who was selected for this game, had to bend over against the wall, to see how many lads could jump on his back. There was Peggy, which was played with a stick and a short square peg, which was tapered at each end. You whacked the peg into the air, when it came down there were numbers on each side of the peg, the highest number face up won, spinning tops was played on the side-walk.

Marbles of course, was another old favourite, which you played in the gutter. There was also Cherry-Wobs, where after you had eaten cherries and kept the stones (the wobs). The game was played by throwing the wobs up the drain spout; the idea being to strike your opponents wob.

A game called Puck was played, with cigarette pack cards. The cigarette packs at that time, had a card in them; there would be footballers, cricket players, steam trains and many more. We would ask the men for them at the Park Street Dockers clearing house (the building were Dockers were selected for work).

The Dockers Pen, as it was commonly known, was like a cattle market; if your face fitted, you were taken on for work. The men stood in a line, and the boss man would literally point, or tap them on the shoulder. Some poor buggers never got a look in. At the pub, some men bought the boss a pint to keep well in. Everybody smoked in those days, so we would ask them, "Any ciggy cards mister?"

To play puck, you would stand your ciggy cards against the wall, while you pucked (flicked) a card between your fingers, to try and knock them down. Cigarette cards, if in complete sets, would normally have 52 cards in a full pack. Full sets would be quite expensive today. We had our favourites… footballers like Dixie Dean, cricketers Wally Hammond, kings of speed Malcolm Campbell, John Cobb, Railways and many more sets.

Then there was a gambling game we played called Bang-Out, which was played by banging your halfpenny against the wall, the next person would also bang his halfpenny against the wall, if he could span with his fingers the two halfpennies, he won. There was Pitch and Toss, where you put any number coins on the palm of your hand and toss them up, then you counted the number of heads and took the coins that were heads. We also played a game called leads, this game consisted of having a number of small inch square pieces of flattened lead of which you marked the pavement into numbered sections,

The leads were thrown from the edge of the street curb. There were also many street gambling games, which were totally unlawful.

Another game we used to play, where everybody joined in, was jumping in the rope. There would be a long rope stretched across the street, as there was hardly any traffic in those days, usually just the occasional doctor's car visiting someone. The mothers would swing the rope, and everyone would jump in the middle of the rope, and all sing the skipping songs, such as, "All in together to see Cinderella, when I count twenty, the rope must be empty." There were many skipping songs, these games created 'Social Tooling'.

One more good game was tying a rope to the top of a gas lamp-post; then you would swing round the lamp-post. The lamp-post was also handy if you were playing cricket, again the lamp-post was also used as the wickets. There was re-allyo, (a game not unlike hide and seek), if those who were hiding reached the den first, they would kick the den wall and shout re-allyo, the seeker would have to be the seeker again.

As in my childhood we had no television, or electronic games, but there was also whip and top, there were many games we played, we made our own amusements.

CHAPTER FOUR

The Best Game, Football

At the time it was 1s3d, to get into a football match. The 27 tram to Anfield, or the number 20 or 3 to Goodison Park, was 3d from the Dingle. You could get into the grounds free after half time, but that ended when the attendances got bigger. Those were the days, when footballers were totally dedicated to their clubs, It was £12 for a win £11 for a draw, and £10 if they lost.

I remember a player in 1947, by the name of Albert Stubbins, who played centre foreward who signed for Liverpool from Newcastle United for a record fee in those days of £13,000, but I thought he was too good for Liverpool. Then there was Cyril Lambert who used to belt the ball from one end of the pitch to the other of the ground. Jacky Balmer was an inside foreward who never got his shorts dirty, but I remember he scored ten goals in three successive matches, which still stands as a record today. He always seemed to look old, as he had a big moustache. Billie Liddell was Liverpool's favourite player, Liverpool was known as the big boot team. During the war years, football teams had guest players. I remember the likes of Matt Busby playing for Liverpool, Billy Steel, Bill Shankley and many more players, keeping up with their profession.

Everton was known as the school of science, with the likes of Tommy Lawton, a great centre forward. He took over after the great Dixie Dean, the player who scored 60 goals in a 38 match season and was one of the most prolific centre forewords in the game. Dean signed for Everton in 1929 from Tranmere Rovers, and finished with Everton in 1938. Everton had the best centre half I ever remembered, T.G Jones, who played in the forties and early fifties.

I remember being at the record gate of 78,000 people, for Everton against Liverpool this was a league game. The largest attendance ever for a cup tie was 118,000 for Everton vs. Liverpool. This came about by having six huge TV screens put up at Liverpool's ground, this was for the supporters who could not get tickets to watch the match at Goodison Park.

I queued up all day for tickets at Goodison Park. The police lost the plot, and instead of allowing the queue to filter into Bullens Road in an orderly fashion, they allowed the whole queue into the Bullens Road, which was not a very wide street. The street was one huge mass of people, a young kid alongside me got his arm broken. I struggled to get out of the queue, my ribs were being crushed, and I never did get a ticket. I had to do with a ticket for the Anfield TV show. There were 70,000 supporters at Goodison and 48,000 at Anfield's ground; this was by far the largest attendance ever for a cup tie.

We would travel to the match by tramcar. The trams would be stretched way back along Spellow Lane. They could get over 90 passengers on the tram, what a squeeze!

Liverpool was known as the big boot up the park, in those days, it was the five, three, two game formation. Everton was the first club to pay wages between seasons, as before the Second World War players had to find work, as other clubs did not pay wages during the closed season.

When I was an apprentice working at Howson's, we had a labourer named Stan Polk. He played for Liverpool as an inside forward; he had to work to supplement his wages. On Saturday mornings, we let him clock off first, as he was playing a game in the afternoon. Stan would have to leg it up Sandhills Lane. Stan was a good player, but not having the right training, he soon tired. There were no £100,000 a week player salaries then, he couldn't earn that money in a lifetime of working.

We British thought we were invincible; after all, we'd taught the game to the rest of the world. But along came the Hungarians in 1953 to show us how to play our game, with the likes of Ferenc Puskas, Hidegkuti and Kocsis. We were amazed at their ball control; and they played us off the park. Our biggest disgrace was before, in 1950, when the U.S.A beat us 1-0. We had our best team playing, internationals such as Mathews, Mortenson and Finny. It took England years to try and catch up.

After 57 years, we still have not reached the standard of many European teams.

However, the best team that I have ever seen was the Brazilian team of 1970, which starred the greatest player whoever played the game - "Pele". They also had Tostow, Gerincha and Santa Maria; the whole team was like watching dream football.

England's finest hour came in 1966, in the World Cup final. We beat West Germany 4-2 at the old Wembley stadium. Since then, we have had some stuttering starts. I may be contradicting myself at this present time, but it must be said the Premier League is the hardest and fastest in football anywhere in the world.

Today the English premiership is now on a par with European football, the only problem is that most of the top players are foreign. However, English football is the better for it. The wages paid to footballers in this country are the highest paid in the world. I, and many others, believe it's getting out of hand; some top class players are receiving £130,000 per week, which some club players don't receive in a year. Referees are frightened to make a mistake by allowing or disallowing a goal, as there can be millions at stake. It's time now to introduce modern technology into the game. The intimidation shown by footballers is getting out of hand. Now, even referees are receiving much better wages. It is alleged they are in the pockets of Sky Television.

As kids we played football for hours on end, if we got two

sides, there could be 20 aside, kicking anything that moved. At the end of the football season, we played cricket in the street, we broke many a window.

I can recall some rather sad tragedies related to football. I remember the big football tragedy at Bolton's ground when they were playing Stoke City during the 1946-1947 season. Someone forced open the side gate, and thousands poured in and squashed the people in the stands behind the goal. The crash barriers were bent over like matchsticks, killing 39 people. It was alleged a man and his son opened the side gate with a jemmy.

But, since then, there have been more football ground tragedies. In 1985, 58 people were burnt to death at Bradford, when the main stand went up in flames. The cause of this disaster was the waste rubbish under the stand, which had not been cleaned. This was a disaster waiting to happen. A lesson was learnt at Bradford. It was covered by the television. The scenes were horrific to see in your own living room.

The biggest tragedy was on the 15th April 1989, at Sheffield Wednesday's ground, Hillsborough. Liverpool was playing Nott's Forest in another cup tie, when 96 people were crushed to death. The way the police handled the event was criminal. Accusations by the police were that the problem was drunkenness, but this proved later to be false. The real culprit was the police officer in charge of the event Chief Inspector Duckenfield. There had been an identical match the previous year, with no problems. But, unlike the previous year, the Liverpool supporters were not allowed to park their cars near the ground this time, but had to park miles away and walk. No attempt was made to request that the referee put the game back another 15 minutes to allow the supporters extra time to get into the ground.

The police had steered the supporters into the tunnel at the middle of the terrace at the Leppings Lane end, but it was already full. Naturally, when the crowd heard the whistle to start the game, they ran into the tunnel, where the poor buggers where already squashed, this made things much worse. The people could go nowhere; they were trapped like rats. The obvious solution was that the police should have opened the gates that led onto the pitch. It was alleged that the policeman in charge, was actually ready to put the dogs on to the supporters. It was like a battlefield, 95 died that day, horribly killed. The 96th victim died much later, after spending many months in a coma. A friend of mine, a Dr John Ashton, jumped on to the pitch, and being a medical man offered his services to the injured and dying.

Granddad Stamper with Rex in the back yard of Dombey Street taken in 1946.

I find that writing this brings tears to my eyes. My son Paul had a ticket for the Leppings Lane terrace that day. I was watching the tragedy unfold on the television; his mum and I were in a state of shock. Then, he phoned us to say he swapped his ticket for a seat in the seating stand. We both cried for joy - he was safe, but a lad he knew died in the Leppings Lane terrace, as was the case with many local families.

Paul and his mates had joined up afterwards, and the first thing on their minds was to get in touch with home. A kind lady let them use her phone. On the following day the lads went back up to Sheffield, with chocolates and flowers to thank the lady.

The bastard paper the Sun, will forever hang its head in shame the way they reported the lies, and filth. They even accused the supporters of urinating on the poor souls laid out, adjacent to the pitch. They never sold many of their papers in Liverpool after that, it took them a long time to apologize, and to say they got it wrong. With cap in hand, they put out an issue to say so, but the paper is still outlawed in Liverpool.

One of the things I don't like, are the ignoramuses who make a mockery out of one of the biggest tragedies in football, especially the sad loss of the Busby Babes. Eight of them were wiped out at Munich in 1958. They were young lads, with the world at their feet. This was heartbreaking news to any football supporter, no matter who you supported.

It can also be said of those who make a mockery of the Hillsborough disaster. In my thinking this is not what we want from football fans. I attended the memorial service at the Liverpool Cathedral for those who died at Hillsborough. Margaret Thatcher, the Prime Minister, came in the side entrance of the Cathedral; she was not the people's favourite.

CHAPTER FIVE

The Travelling Salesman

I remember the light cake man, who would carry a basket on his head, touting his wares. Another man had a strange contraption on his bike. He would put his bike on a stand, sit back on the saddle connected to a grindstone on the front handlebars, and he would pedal like hell to turn it and sharpen implements against the wheel. He'd shout, "Scissors to grind?" and would also sharpen your knives.

Another attraction was the mobile Merry-go-round, which was drawn by a horse, at 1d a ride.

There was a little Indian man with a tiny hand bell, shouting, "Indian silk toffee!" There was also the tipster, who would shout, "I gave you the winner of the Lincoln!" There were some great characters, back then.

There were many dairymen selling milk from milk floats pulled by a small pony; there was Baines, Thwaites, and Morgan's. There were also handcarts selling sterilised milk called County Pallatine, this milk would have an oily taste but it would last much longer than fresh milk.

On Sundays there would be buskers at the back entry, singing, "Marther rambling rose of the wild rose," or some other ditty. If my mother had a copper to spare, we'd throw it over the backyard wall. Some days there was a line of men, with signs round their necks saying, 'World War One veterans, please give generously!" They would walk in the gutter, one behind the other, busking. I think they were called 'The Foo-Foo Band'. Their instruments were ocarinas and combs blown through tissue paper. God knows what song they were playing; only they knew.

We had some laughs as we kids followed behind them in the gutter. We were told, in no uncertain manner, to "Piss off!" There was a pitch-toss at the bottom of our street. The men would form a circle to gamble. As it was illegal to gamble in public, they would have to have lookouts to raise the alarm if the police were coming. In the ring they had a belt-man, whose job was to keep the ring open. If the ring of men was closing in, he would swing his belt around their knees. They would soon jump back. The rule of pitch and toss was you spin two pennies from your hand if they landed with two heads he won. Two tails he lost.

Believe me gambling on the street was a serious offence. Some policemen could be brutal. One policeman was nicknamed 'Black Rider'. As I remember, one time he battered one unfortunate poor bugger over the head so much that there was blood everywhere. This man was then thrown in the police van, more commonly known as the 'Black Maria' and taken to Essex Street Bridewell. He was thrown into a cell overnight and taken the next day to Dale Street Court. He was fined five pounds. He must have been a right villain, to these narrow-minded thinkers!

It was also illegal to bet on the horses, other than on the racetrack. There were street bookies who would stand on the corner of the street; they'd also employed a lookout. One bookie in Northumberland Street named Button Lacy always gave you a tip when you gave him your bet.

At the end of the day when the last race had finished, you had to go to the bookie's house to get your winnings. He would sit at the kitchen table, check your winning bet and pay you out. You would have to go out the back yard exit, so as not to draw attention to the house. Every so often, the police would catch the bookie. He would be fined £5. He'd pay his fine, then it was business as usual.

The summer months seemed to go on forever; we were never out of the park. It was great rolling down the fields, which are still there today. We use to try and catch tadpoles in Prince's Park Lake. There was a gated area at the entrance to the private gardens, where you had to be accompanied with an adult if you would like to enter. There were beautiful shows of flowers dotted about in this area, so the rule was to protect the flowers from vandalism. Park keepers roamed the park in those days. Princes Park was the first public park built in 1842, but it only became public in the early 1920s, until then it was totally private. It had beautiful gates at the entrances in Princes Road and Belvedere Road and Ullet Road.

It was exciting to go to Speke Airport and see the two-winged aircraft, flying off to far away places like the Isle of Man. This airport was fairly new as it opened in 1933. It was built before the modern Manchester International Airport. The new name of Speke airport is "John Lennon Airport", which is becoming very popular.

My mother would often send me on an errand to Fairy's, the bakers, to get a loaf of bread. The baker would weigh the bread, and if the bread was under-weight he gave you a jockey (a piece of cake) to make up the weight. I always ate this before I got home! Most groceries served loose goods. Today the fancy packaging must help put up the prices of goods.

One shop, called Lipton's, which was a nationwide outlet sold tea loose. Lee's was a shop that sold footwear in Park Road. I think the leather was cardboard, as the boots would wear out in no time. We used to like going to the herbal beer shop. The shop had bunches of different herbs hanging from the ceiling, and they also sold 'sticky-lice' which looked like a twig of wood, and was in fact the root of the liquorice tree which was dug up, washed and chewed as a mouth freshener This was a good thing for keeping your bowels open. The top selling beverage was sarsaparilla. The shop had seats like a café; it was a great meeting place.

Most street traders used horses and carts to carry their wares. The milkman sold his milk straight out of the churn; he would ladle a pint or a gill into your jug or basin. When the coalman called one day, me mam told him off, as she had just scrubbed the kitchen floor. He had to come through the house to throw the bag of coal in the yard. The mess was worse if it had been raining. He said, "Sorry, Mary," bummed a cup of tea, and then had the cheek to ask for a bucket of water for the horse.

Sugar was also sold loose, scooped from a big sack into a blue measured bag. There was a shop opposite our house called Coonie Watt's. It was a general store, and she sold everything, veg, meat, cigs, and she was also a money-lender. Coonies shop was a regular meeting place for all the women. I remember there was a Mrs. Bennett, who was a very strange woman who had a moustache. I think she was foreign. She would say to Mrs. Watts, "A quarter bacon for ham!" To her, ham was meant him; it was just her way of saying it! For an old penny, you could buy old fruit, known as 'fades', before it was dumped.

Prices were related to the earnings, in those times. Food prices had to be low to be in relation to the wages you got. However, that's if you had a job to go to! For example, bread 2d, potatoes 2d a pound and margarine was 3d for half a pound. If you wanted, the grocer would cut the margarine into two pieces, which was only 3 half pence per piece. Meat was always mutton, and was 10d per pound. Meat was kept for Sunday only. If there was any left, we'd have it for our Monday evening meal. This would be a fry-up called 'Pip Squeak'. You could also buy a halfpenny worth of sweets at Coonie Watt's, or on the way there call into Ted's the greengrocer for a penny worth of fades. We'd cut the bad bits off and eat the old fruit.

CHAPTER SIX

Going to the Pictures

Our great treat was going to the pictures. There would be a Saturday matinee on at the Beresford, or the Gaumont or Park Palace. I did like the old Park Palace. We'd see the cowboys Tom Maynard, Buck Jones, Tim McCoy, Flash Gordon and many more. Other cinemas were not so good. There was a particular fleapit called the Warwick, and the Jamie in Park Lane had no balcony.

In the city centre there were many theatres, the Empire, Hippodrome, Shakespeare, Pavilion, and the Rotunda on Scotland Road. The Williamson Square Playhouse which has great character, was built in mid-1866, and was called the "Star Theatre". The Theatre is the oldest repertory theatre in the country. The 'Redgrave's' started their stage careers there along with Richard Todd and Rex Harrison and many more. On one side of the square there was a beautiful building, the "Theatre Royal," which was built around the 1770s and closed in the 1880s, and used later as a cold store, but you could pick out the grandeur of the building, alas is no more. The Liverpool sports shop, an ugly building, now stands on the site.

The Everyman Theatre in Hope Street is now a great, flourishing theatre. It originated as a church called the Hope Hall Mission, then at the end of the 19th century it became a cinema and kept its name the Hope Hall which closed as a cinema in the early sixties. Then it became a theatre, renamed the Everyman. Its partner the Playhouse is even more famous.

As a kid, I remember looking at the prices on the board

outside the Playhouse. The prices started at 9d to be in the gallery, up to £1/16/6 for the box seats. To me as a kid, those prices were very expensive.

We also saw silent films, as talkies had only been out for about six years. Even today, I still love these silent films, starring the likes of Laurel and Hardy, Charley Chaplin, Buster Keaton, the Marx Brothers, the Three Stooges, Edgar Kennedy and Ben Turpin, just to mention a few. Halfway through the film, the attendant would come up and down the aisles, spraying everything with his Flit gun. This was supposed to keep the germs down. If the projector broke down, there would be uproar. Everyone would bang their feet on the floor, until the problem was solved. When it was, a big cheer would go up as the film came back on.

If we had no money, we would sneak in via the back door, with the aid of our mates on the inside. The Park Palace, known affectionately as the Ace, was originally a theatre. It was built in 1893 and during the late 1890s, live acts were performed. Seating in the Palace was a gallery with large steps. At the back of the gallery, an eight-inch board ran around. At the centre, the seating dropped down a foot to allow the film to be projected onto the screen. Often, somebody would put their hands up, and make shapes with their fingers, which was displayed on the screen. A great shout would go up, "Put your bloody hands down!"

The circle had just two rows. There were plush seats, but the seat was simply a continuous bench running from one end of the circle to the other. If more people wanted to come in, the commissioner would make you move up. We'd have to squash up, and kids in the gallery would be pulling our hair, since we were only about a foot below the gallery. The Palace also had two boxes on each side, as it had earlier been a theatre. This was where canoodling took place!

The stalls, or the pit area, had seat forms. With just five rows at the front of the cinema, these were the only proper seats in the house. It was too bad if you had to sit in the front seats, the characters in the film seem to be walking down a hill. Sometimes there would be a shout from the usher, "Keep that baby quiet!". Today, it is still in good condition. After the cinema closed in 1957, later it was used as a chemist, and then a motor engineering shop. I am not sure what they are going to do with the theatre!

Recently some theoretical historical organisation did a research in the Park Palace, and found hidden behind the walls and ceiling panels were beautiful original constructed designs in plaster work. What is to become of it, I do not know?

It was 3d to go to the Beresford, and the same price for the Gaumont. The Gaumont was a very good cinema. They had an organ that came up from the pit, the organist was Harold Themes. The Warwick was only 1d, but it was a flea pit. When they opened the Mayfair, it was posh. There were lights at each row. The Wurlitzer organ came up from the pit, and the whole of the organ was lit up.

There were many ways of getting your entrance money. You could sell jam jars to Packenhams or Larry Kings the scrap merchants, a penny for a big jar, halfpenny for a small jar. The prices to go into the Palace cinema at the evening performance was 6d in the gallery, 9d in the circle, 9d on the bench seats in the stalls, and 10d to sit on proper seats in the stalls The cinemas would show films Monday to Wednesday, then different films Thursday to Saturday. Most nights they showed two films, the first film being a B category, or maybe a comedy followed by the 'main film'.

Children were not allowed in the cinema unless they were with an adult – so you would have to stand outside the cinema asking grownups to "Take us in, Mister?" There is no way you can do that today.

I remember helping one of the lads who got a job working for Lunt's Bread Delivery, Dave Jameson. This was in St Mary's

Road, Aigburth. His work was pushing a bread van around the leafy roads of Aigburth. The van had two wheels and a large covered box with two little doors. If it was raining, I would climb in amongst the bread where it was warm. Dave would give me a shilling for helping him.

On the front page of the *Liverpool Echo* newspaper there was an index of three rows of cinemas. There were maybe fifty cinemas in all. Liverpool had two evening papers; the other paper was the Evening Express. The price was 1d, the Sunday papers were 2d, and the better papers were 3d. I remember the paper man, Albert Horne. He was blind, and was a short stubby man. His change was always correct.

CHAPTER SEVEN

Great Adventures

It was a lovely sight to see the illuminated tram going up Park Road, lit up with hundreds of electric lights. They had a band aboard, and people dressed up in 'Pierriot' costumes. As kids we would sit on the corner of Byles Street and Park Road, starry-eyed as the tram passed by.

We used to sit outside the Dingle Station, where we would put bottle tops on the tramlines. The tram would flatten them and when you retrieved them, they would fit neatly into the chocolate machine.

Our houses were lit by gaslights. You had to light the gas mantle, which was very fragile. It cost 3 half pence to buy, and was in a little cardboard box. If the gas was running down, you had to put a penny in. You had good warning, as the gaslights would gradually grow dimmer, which would give you a chance to find a penny to put in the slot.

Every so often the gasman came to empty the meter. He would tip the contents onto the table. There would be maybe ten shillings or 120 old pence, in pennies. My mam might get a 2/- rebate, and if she did, she gave Eddy and me 2d each. Some people used to rob, or 'borrow', breaking into their gas meters when they really needed money.

I remember the time, when I was about 7 years of age, a mate of mine called Billy Millington and I where in Prince's Park. It would have been nearly 5pm, going dusk, when we heard the Park Police whistle being blown. It was Mr. Foulks the park-keeper, a very severe-looking man with a big moustache. We feared him. In all the parks, whistles were blown as a warning to leave before the gates were closed for the night, as the parks were only open from dawn to dusk.

Billy said the he knew of a short cut out of the park. We did not want to get caught by 'Foulksy', but as we climbed over the back of St Paul's churchyard, my foot got stuck in a bent railing. I tried to jump but my head hit the railings, and a spike nearly went in my eye. I was wailing my head off, and Billy did a runner. Mr. Foulks arrived and lifted me off the railings, as gentle as can be. He changed from someone I feared, into just another human being. He carried me to the number 25 tram, then took me up to the Children's Hospital in Myrtle Street. He then sent for my mother.

I was in hospital for five days. After that, I always respected Mr. Foulks. There used to be railings around all the parks, but they took them all away for scrap, to help with the war effort. However, most of the railings were not used and just left to rot. They were never replaced after the war. That is a pity, because that might have stopped the vandals from wrecking the parks.

The Prince's Park gates at the Belvedere Road entrance were very ornate, and built by expert craftsmen. These were beautiful gates called "Sunburst", I believe they are replacing them, but the gates in front of the Sailors' Home in Canning Place were a work of art. I read that a Birmingham scrap yard now has the gates, used as an entrance to their yard, and Liverpool Council is trying to buy them back. I recently wrote to the West Bromwich Council regarding the gates, and they wrote me a nice letter back to say that the Liverpool Council can have them back, providing they have them listed, and maintained.

At Christmas time, we kids would go carolling to the posh houses in the Aigburth area. You could receive as much as a shilling, and we would share the money out. I later came across a shopping pamphlet from 1936, which belonged to Mary, my mother-in-law. She sadly died in 1975. It was called the 'Liverpool Suburbia Shopping Guide'. There were shops with items and prices, for example, 'J.W.Coats, Park Road: Socks,

1/- (15p) a pair'. At R&P Cycles it was £2/19/11, in today's money 299p for a bicycle, or at Kennedy's Chemist you could buy a pint of cod liver oil for 1/6 (7½p). There was an interesting article advertising that The Hospital Association of Merseyside could provide private accommodation in hospital for 1/- a week. There was no N.H.S. in those days; if you wanted to see the doctor, you had to pay.

A custom we had in the south of Liverpool in the thirties was burning Judas. This would take place on Good Friday, very early in the morning. We would spend weeks getting any old rubbish together. We'd raid other gangs' stores of rubbish and make an effigy of Judas. We'd stick him on top of the fire, which was then lit. I have no idea how this custom started, but it had a religious context, I think it started in the nineteenth century. This custom should not be confused with the burning of Guy Fawkes, which normally took place on November the 5th. The custom of burning Judas was only known in the south end of the city. We never had trick or treat in my day. This is a daft idea, which came from the United States.

There was a time when my mother decided that Eddy and I should become Roman Catholics. She'd take us up to Mount Carmel to see the priest for instruction. I clearly remember one Sunday Mass at Our Lady of Mount Carmel in High Park Street. Not being fully converted to the faith at the time, our kid and I were at the rear of the church. Suddenly the school headmaster took both of us by the ear lobes, and dragged us to the altar for communion. Realizing his mistake, he dragged us back to our seats. My mother was appalled at his actions. That was the end of our conversion. Although my mother was a Catholic, she could never take Communion, as she was married outside of the faith.

Altogether, it was nearly twenty years before I converted. It was through my own verification that I accepted the faith, but I certainly question some of the doctrines today. I still question my faith.

CHAPTER EIGHT

Brunswick Gardens

We left 67, Byles Street in May of 1938. All the furniture had to be stoved at Coleman's Warehouse to prevent any vermin going into the new house. Our new home was to be Brunswick Gardens.

This was a set of tenements, which was situated between Park Street and Northumberland Street, Caryl Street and Grafton Street. Our number was 20a. There were three blocks of tenements which ran along Caryl Street, in which they were four landings high. We lived in the middle block, on the first landing. There was a two landings block, and a neighbouring block was the pensioners' accommodations.

At Brunswick Gardens, our hall was square and we had two bedrooms and the living room was an eating-come living room. The back kitchen led off the living room, and also in the hall was the door for a tiny bathroom. There was a coal store, the back kitchen was about eight feet square. My mother had to go to the Steble Street wash house to wash the clothes. I had to help carry the tin bath with two handles. It was O.K. carrying the washing up Park Street, when it was dry, but coming back when the washing was wet, it was much heavier to carry. The only way to dry the clothes was on a line hung over the landing wall. It was too bad when an item of clothing fell down; I had to dash down the landing stairs to retrieve it, but it was worse for those on the top landing, rushing down eight flights of stairs! I could not understand why the council placed people with large families on the top landing flats. Some of the families had as many as eight or ten children.

My Father Edmund Army 1942

However, we thought we were in dreamland. No more gaslight! There were switches on the wall to give us electricity. We bought an electric radio. No more going to Radio-Vim for an acid bottle (accumulator) or a big Ever-Ready battery as the old wireless had to be wired-up, to tune into the radio. It was a common sight to see lads going shopping up to Mill Street. It was the done thing, calling in to Billy Millers the butcher, with your ration books.

The war years are a time that most of us who lived through will never forget. During these dark years of wartime, the pub was a haven, an escape. I remember during the war a stick of incendiary bombs falling in the Northumberland Street block. The only way to extinguish these bombs was with sand, as they were phosphorus. A woman on the top landing started to throw buckets of water over the landing and soaked the poor air raid wardens who were dealing with the situation, we thought it was hilarious.

The war years believe me, we had some exciting times, it was not all gloom and doom. Most of the men were away in forces, my father included. At this time he was in Egypt in the Army. My mother started to go out in the evenings, and she eventually brought home a young Belgium seaman who was much younger than her.

At first, Eddy and I were very naïve about the affair. They slept together, and this went on for some time. However, during the war years, there were many young women who were having affairs. It was a case of 'when the cat's away, the mice will play'. This type of thing was going on throughout the country, but when I look back, it was not an experience for a twelve year old kid to go through. Some years later, I realized there was no love between my parents. I suppose to my mother, this gave her licence to do what she wanted to do, like playing around or having a fling.

However, like the old saying, it takes two to tango. My father came back from the war in 1945 and the atmosphere between my parents was really tense.

A year later, we moved from Brunswick Gardens to Tiber Street. Shortly after we moved (I was about 16 years old), my mother left home to live with Wilfy Yates. She'd known him since before the war, he was a Manx man and she lived in the Isle of Man. But after a while, she returned to Liverpool.

During this time, I stayed living at home with my father. A short time after my mother left home, my father brought home a young woman. She had been on the game, or so I heard.

I couldn't accept this woman. They had a child. I can't remember whether it was a girl or a boy, as after a very short time the baby died in the bed in which my father and this woman slept. There was an inquest, the verdict was accidental death.

This period was the most miserable time of my life. I used the house only to sleep in; going to work was my escape from the existence I experienced at home. I would have to get up at 6.30am, as I had to catch the overhead train from the Dingle to get to the Huskerson dock for 7.30am. You worked a five and a half day week in the forties. I would cycle to the overhead railway where for 1 pence a day, you could leave your bike in the little station's lock-up. As I was always in a hurry, I would leap off my bike outside the bike shed, the bike would find its own way into the bike shed. As I was getting my ticket, I could hear the bike parking itself. In those days the train ticket was 7 pence, workman's return. When I finished work, I never went straight home. I used to go to my mates, Chris White's house in Essex Street, where his mother usually gave me my evening meal. After all these trials and tribulations, what I feel for my parents now is sadness. In the early years of their marriage back in the twenties and thirties, the older generation would have a saying, "You made your bed, now lay in it".

This reflects the sad way of the times, although today the thought of marriage is becoming like a football. People today live together, which makes it easier to split up for the most stupid things. I find in today's way of thinking that there is no thought of a commitment to one another.

Divorce would have been harder to get in my parents' day. If it was the same situation today, my parents would have been well divorced.

I learnt at an early age, the pitfalls of my parents' marriage, and this is a testament to the success of my own marriage. But I never hated my parents; they sadly ruined their own lives. I can say now, that after 49 years of my marriage, I have no regrets. I still have the same feelings for my wife Eileen as when we were first married, probably more so.

My mother returned to Tiber Street one evening with Wilfy and his brother to take away some furniture. Wilf's brother George had a lock-up in St Anne's Street. They took some items, including her sideboard, but I can't remember what else. There was one almighty row. One angry word led to another, and then my mother whacked my father over the head with the poker. I ran into the backyard with my mother. My father threw a milk bottle at the window at my mother and I in the yard, the bottle came straight through the glass, and it hit me on the head, in which I was slightly stunned and had a small cut. I think my dad was very shocked when he realized what he had done, he was apologetic to me. I had been the piggy in the middle, as my brother Eddy was away in the army, it was many years before I met him again.

I eventually went to live with my grandmother, on my mother's side, in Dingle Mount. Living in my grandmothers at that time was my granddad Harry, Joey, the eldest son of my grandparents, and Jimmy, the three of them were all dockers. Tommy the other son worked for Shell-Mex.

Therefore it was a very male orientated household, I remember granddad always sat on a cane chair, by the fire smoking his pipe. He had a terrible habit of spitting into the fire, with sound of (tish) as it hit the fire bars. Granddad would always reminisce about his tales in Egypt during the 1st World War, of which we all have heard the same tale before. Even grandma would have to check the story to put him on the right track. He would say "who is bloody telling this tale me or you?" It was like a pantomime,

Granddad, after working in the docks for over 60 years, was presented with a medal, he threw it in the fire saying "the lousy bastards". I don't blame him, after toiling all those years. There was no pension paid in those days, it was a hard life. Between the three of them they had put in more than 130 years between them, Granddad died in 1959 and Grandma followed him in 1960; she had a very hard life.

CHAPTER NINE

Just Before the War

In our old house in Byles Street, we had had to boil a kettle on the fire for hot water. In our new house in Brunswick Gardens, there was a Work-Well fire grate that heated the hot water. The council never fitted radiators in the houses. I don't think the coal man was very happy carrying the bags of coal up to the top landing, eight flights of stairs. We were lucky we lived on the first landing. Living in Brunswick Gardens was a steep learning curve. You became streetwise and learnt to stand on your own feet. We had great fun - the dock road was our playground. Sometimes for fun we would jump on wagons, this would be a normal pastime, known as skips. During the school holidays, we would make our way down to the dock road, jump on a skip to the Custom House in Canning Square.

Our coalman had a horse and cart, like most tradesmen in those days. The bin wagon was also horse drawn. The Corporation had some beautiful horses, which were well looked after. There was a good system for loading and unloading bin wagons. The container for taking the rubbish away was an enclosed wagon, with four small wheels, and the front of the wagon sloped down. When this was full, the horse was taken from the full wagon, then they brought up a big lorry with an empty spare container.

The driver would come round to the back of the lorry and pull out two steel plates, channel shaped.

The wagon was a tipper so they would lower the empty container by means of a hydraulic lift and heavy cables, down the steel channels, then the full wagon was hauled back up the same way. The horse was backed up into the empty wagon. The full wagon was then returned to the refuse yard in Wellington Road where the refuse was burnt. There was no recycling in those days; everything was burnt.

There was another firm of carters, called "Larry Marr's". They had some of the best Shire horses in the country. What a sight it was to see these horses during the May Day parades! They'd parade through town, all the horse brasses gleaming, the horses' coats were brushed and clipped, all the carts freshly painted. All the carting firms vied with each other for first prize. The carters treated their horses as if they were human. Before they had there own dinner, they fed the horse first. I remember one word used only by carters was 'Gamer', which was a friendly greeting they'd call out to one another.

My mother would have to wash the small clothes in the sink, if she didn't have a lot of clothes to wash. If it was a large wash of clothes, it would have to be the washhouse in Steble street. Like most people, we had no washing machine, although we did have a bathroom. Some people I knew had pet mice in the bath, and others stored coal in the bath.

There were some characters living in 'Brunny', as we called Brunswick Gardens. Our next-door neighbour made her husband take off his boots before he was allowed in. Her house was like a palace. One of the problems with the flats was they were not sound proofed at all. If there was a party going on in the flat above, you would be in for it. The ceiling would shake, We used a brush pole to bang on the ceiling.

On the outside landings, there was a chute located between the flats. You pulled a small steel door open and you threw your trash through the hole in the wall, the trash would fall down a big pipe to a bin at the bottom of the flats, from where the bin men removed it weekly. It was too bad for the tenants who lived on the ground floor adjacent to the bin. They had to keep their back kitchen window shut, as the bottom bin door had no seal, the dust would fly all over the place.

The flats employed a caretaker, a Mr. Gosling. Every day he'd clean the nine sets of stairways of the blocks with his hosepipe and wash the stairs down, with a yard brush from top to bottom. This practice came to halt when war broke out, and throughout the war, the tenements were very unkempt. Standards slipped in the council and no money was spent in the upkeep of the flats; the stairs smelt of urine. Before the war, all the verandas had had geraniums growing in little recesses in the wall, but now the little bushes have also gone.

There was great demand for more council housing, but the council did not have a coherent planning strategy for building. The planners thought they'd build upwards, as this saved space and was cheaper. They also tried to justify this by saying that blocks of flats created a closer knit society. However, building flats created slums. There were too many old properties still standing, most of which were slums, which could have been redeveloped.

Today, most of the flats are gone, but nearly half the population of Liverpool has been moved to the outside of the Liverpool's boundaries. The city has lost a large portion of its income from rates. 300,000 is nearly half the population, this would be an awful lot of people to lose. I think what Liverpool needs today is re-population. The council moved many people to places like Skelmesdale, Widnes, Runcorn, Winsford and Kirkby.

Before the war, different nationalities lived in different areas of Liverpool. For example, the area between Hurst Street and Carpenter's Row was where the Spanish lived, Pitt Street and Kent Street is where the Chinese lived, and have lived in this area for the past 150 years as this was the oldest Chinese area in Europe. The West Africans and West Indians resided in Stanhope and Berkeley Streets; the Arabs lived mostly in Park

Lane; the Italians lived in Soho Street and in around the Gerard Gardens area. There was a strong contingent of Irish people living in the Scotland Road area. This made Liverpool a city of many nationalities.

The area where I lived, Northumberland, Warwick and Hill Streets, lived mostly Catholics, and Park Street and Essex Street were mainly Protestant. Jewish people lived in the areas of Islington and Brownlow Hill. Unfortunately, on the 12th of July there was always conflict between the Catholics and the Protestants. Unlike Manchester, it got quite nasty at times, on both sides.

However, some good has come out of this, as these run down areas were demolished during the 50s and 60s. Since so many people were moved to other areas of Liverpool, things are much quieter now.

There were lots of young kids who lived in 'Brunnie'. We formed a gang and we had some great times. Caryl Street was our footie pitch, where there may be as many as 15 a side. It got so crowded that you could not see the ball for legs kicking, but it was great fun.

Two of us were charged by the police for playing football in the street, but we were let off with a caution. The judge was angry with the policeman for wasting time and public money.

There were no proper playing fields near us. Some days, mainly at weekends, the men would play a match in Caryl Street. It cost 2/- a man to take part, with the proceeds going to the winning side. Usually, there was a big set to, so bad that the police would come and a few players got carted off to Essex Street Bridewell. Some of these men were nearly of conscription age, and a few weeks away from their call up, but they were treated like real criminals!

Opposite our flats was the Fever Hospital. Running along Caryl Street to Warwick Street was Warwick Gardens. On the opposite side of the street was Caryl Gardens, these flats ran to Hill Street and opposite the flats was the Royal Southern hospital at Hill Street.

I had my cartilage removed at the Southern Hospital by a surgeon called Mr McFarland, brother to a well known figure at the Magistrate courts. He was the Stipend Judge who was situated in Dale Street, who could put fear into those who came before him.

CHAPTER TEN

Camping Money

One summer the gang decided to earn some money so we could go camping. There would be about twelve of us on the trip. Coal was rationed, but we knew where to find it. There was a high wall along the Cheshire Lines Railway, and on the other side was a deep cutting to the railway. It had about a 40-foot drop. We decided to lower ropes, and some of us would climb down the ropes and collect coal that had dropped off the steam engines. After we filled the sacks with coal, we'd haul the coal up from the cutting, and sell it off at 6p a bag. Unbeknown to us, the coal was steam coal and you could not burn it in an ordinary fire-grate. It had to be burnt in a steam engine with a forced draft, but we still sold it.

By the time the warmer weather came, we had enough cash, which one of the lads had looked after. The luckier lads had proper tents, and those who didn't, made one out of canvas and a couple of brush poles. This was very D.I.Y, but worked to a fashion.

Our transport was our bikes. No two bikes were alike. George Ratchford's bike was a 28inch which was the largest bike made. My bike was a sit-up-and-beg, some called it a nurses bike, with a dropped and bent cross bar. I bought this bike for the princely sum of 6p and a big bottle of lemonade. Gerry Larkin was the only one who had a real bike. It was a racer, how we envied his bike!

We loaded up the bikes with the essentials, and pedalled to maybe the other side of Chester. We begged a farmer for some water, until he tired of us and chased us away.

#4 Hatch

One of George's pedals came off his bike halfway through the Mersey Tunnel and he had to push his bike the rest of the way through. In those days, hardly any traffic would use the tunnel on Sundays, so they allowed cyclists to use the tunnel at weekends free. The road surface of the Mersey Tunnel was very dangerous as it had a steel surface with diamond shaped studs. If any oil dropped on the road, vehicles would skid.

Some years ago, they closed the branch tunnel that left the main tunnel to go through to Wallasey. You can still see the opening today on your right, as you approach Birkenhead exit. However, I don't think, or considered the volume of traffic that would build up. Traffic lights stopped the flow of traffic, and even at that time it caused traffic jams. The conclusion was to close the branch tunnel forever; whoever designed the branch from Wallasey to run into the main Birkenhead tunnel should never be allowed near a drawing board.

Many years later when Eileen and I with the four kids were returning home from Eileen's sisters house in Wallasey and coming through the tunnel from the Wallasey entrance, the traffic lights where on red on the entrance to the main tunnel. The bloody car was doing tricks, didn't want to start. As soon as green came on, here's me outside the car pushing like hell. The engine came alive, I jumped in the car - no way am I paying £10 to have it towed out, we got home OK.

The branch tunnel is now used as an escape tunnel. The Mersey Tunnel has to have pumps going 24 hours a day, otherwise the tunnel would be flooded in no time. The pumps therefore have to run 24 hours a day, and there are secondary, stand-by pumps in case of pump breakdown. At one time, they came up with the idea of using the bottom part of the tunnel for tram cars. However, this was impossible as there is always water in that part of the tunnel.

The Runcorn Bridge is another place where there are frequent traffic jams. They built the bridge with only three lanes. Again, where was the foresight? Now they have to build another bridge further east, which is going to cost £380 million pounds. When the new bridge is finished, both bridges will have tolls.

I remember in the fifties before the bridge, the only crossing was the old Transporter that crossed from Widnes to Runcorn. This contraption was a suspended box hung on steel cables above the Mersey River and the Manchester Ship Canal. This was demolished in the early sixties. I only used it once when I took Eileen for a spin on my Lambretta scooter, just before we got married.

Eileen and I had an accident on the Southport Road. We were doing about 45mph when the front tyre burst, I couldn't control the scooter, we were both were flung off into the road, and by the grace of God, there were no cars following behind us. I think Eileen had second thoughts at going out again on the scooter.

CHAPTER ELEVEN

My First Job

I have already mentioned, around this time I started work. I had left school at 14 years of age. The school was situated at the bottom of Stanhope Street, opposite Higson's Brewery and warehouses; you could smell the hops and spices in the school yard. The school was Harrington Council School, which unfortunately was for those destined for the factories (factory fodder). We didn't even sit the 11-plus exam; there was no possibility of further education.

My first job when I left school was in Percy Street, off Canning Street, where all the beautiful Georgian houses were built. The house was very large and had a huge basement, where we had the workshop. I started as an electrical engineer and my pay was 7/6d for a 48 hour week. We made press button starters for machines.

My father told me to pack up the job due to the long hours and low pay, so I left after a short time.

I got a job working in a garage. The foreman asked me to clean the toilets but I said, "No way, give me my cards!" I worked there for only two weeks. I next worked for a jobbing outfit, based in the back yard of a small terraced house in Speakland Road. We had to push a big handcart loaded with two long ladders and buckets, cement and slates. We were sent to a job off Scotland Road, about six miles away, to replace a couple of roof slates to the outside toilet, Once again, this job was going nowhere.

The man I worked with liked his ale, he was cross-eyed (or

one home and one away), so I had to sit waiting on the cart freezing cold, while he was in the pub. My wage was £1/10s. I soon packed this job in. The man thought we should just leave the cart in a back street off Scotland Road, so that's what we did. He said to me, sod the employer and his bloody ladders! We got our cards. The employer had a fit when he asked us, what have you done with the ladders?

My next job was at Jameson's Ships fender makers.

This job entailed making rope fenders. We worked in Argyle Street, in a seven storey high, 18th century warehouse. The firm had two other warehouses; one in Bridgewater Street and one in Cornwallis Street. Jameson's employed about 300 lads under the army conscription age of eighteen years. This being war time, the work came under the Essential Works Act.

We each had a wooden barrel. The top had been removed and the barrel filled with waste sacking. This enabled you to sit the pudding fender in the barrel, before the coir rope was half-hitched to the side of the raw fender. The finished fender was made up of half hitches. My brother Eddy also worked at the same time at Jameson's, but he was at Bridgwater Street warehouse.

Eddy in two years had over twenty jobs. Mr Jameson had one leg he got around on crutches. One day our Eddy had a almighty row with Mr Jameson, then during the argument our kid thought that he was in for a beating off old Jamo, he grabbed his crutches off him, making him legless, I believe it was like a pantomime. Our Eddy was a swine, he was not frightened of anyone, all the lads jeered him on. One day Mr Jameson was out of the office for a short time, and while he was away a couple of lads pinched the safe. When old Jamo came back to the office, he gave them an ultimatum by saying I am going out of the office for a half hour and if the safe is not back I will have the police in. The safe was put back pronto. The old bugger knew how to handle the lads.

Our Eddy has had some nasty injuries, he worked for Leatherans, a scrap metal site. One time he was lifting some metal with a hand winch, while he was turning the handle he slipped, the handle spun backwards, and it caught him in the face, with no remuneration. He would have certainly have been compensated in today's society, Another job where he was injured was in a warehouse where there was a hoist that had a large heavy ball and hook, he playing silly buggers pretending to head it, as you would head a case ball, but the iron ball struck him, and knocked him out cold. He came home, with a black eye as his left eye was completely closed. He was hard as nails, and sometimes he made you laugh. He was a bugger at times.

Working in Jameson's you worked piecework, which meant you were paid according to the number of fenders you had made at the end of the day. The pay was 1/6d for an ordinary fender, 1/9d for a hard laid fender and 2/6d for a sausage fender, which was used for landing barges. You could earn good money in Jameson's, £3 to £5 pounds a week. If you worked hard all day, you could turn out 8 fenders. Our hands were like leather from using the coir rope all day.

I worked on the fifth floor in the Argyle Street warehouse. Opposite our building was the Argyle Street Bridewell. Since this was wartime, it had been taken over by the military. We used to watch the army deserters and Germans who had been shot down taken into the Bridewell. They were then sent off to prison camps.

One day, we watched one of the English prisoner's literally squeeze himself up out of a manhole cover in the middle of the road. It was a very tight squeeze, and he finally popped out the manhole like a cork. We didn't let on what was going on. He was probably an army deserter, sent down to the cellar to shovel the coal. After about half an hour, they realized he was missing. It was like something from the 'Keystone Cops'. They shouted up to us, asking which way he had gone. We sent them on a wild goose chase, telling them he had gone up Duke Street, when in fact he had gone down Paradise Street. We all had a good laugh!

One day we found a box of reject Durex condoms, since our warehouse was next to the Airton & Saunders factory. We went up to the top floor, where we blew them up and sent them off to blow over the city centre.

Today, most of these buildings are fancy restaurants. They took five storeys off the top of the building I worked in, and made a classy restaurant. The Argyle Bridewell is a restaurant, but the building has not been altered. Even the cells have been kept, and are used as snugs to drink in. I am glad they saved these parts of old Liverpool. At the bottom of Hanover and Duke Streets, they have saved three more beautiful buildings. Unfortunately, they couldn't save Cassertelly's wine importers, but there is still a similar building at the apex of Hanover and Duke Streets. This whole area has the classical feeling of old Liverpool, as it was in the 18th and 19th centuries.

They have saved a number of Georgian and Victorian buildings in this area, at the bottom of Hanover Street, such as the old seamen's mission and the other buildings opposite. The old Bluecoat building has been furnished to its original splendour.

I remember the terrible fire at Henderson's building in Church Street, where there was a number of deaths. The fire started in the kitchens which was situated in the upper floors. I remember as the fire raged, a man was helping customers along the ledge on top of the building, the man saved many lives, but sadly he fell from the building and lost his own life, what a hero.

Coopers' shop in Church Street sold coffee, the coffee was being roasted in the little side street. The aroma that was emanated from the coffee was lovely. There was Woolworths in Church Street which was the first Woolworths to come out of America, making it the first Woolworths in Europe.

During these times Church Street was a very busy street, the side walks were bustling with people and there were two police men stopping the traffic, which was mainly trams, to allow the people to cross to the other side of the street.

This was one of the places we would frequent. This picture is taken from the end of Park Lane, looking towards the beautiful Custom House, where you could walk through the three archways and come out at South Castle Street, second greatest building to St George's Hall. Many happy times were spent in this vicinity.

CHAPTER TWELVE

The War Years

As I mentioned before, the Cheshire Lines warehouse was opposite our flats. When one of the big doors was open, we didn't think twice. Quick as a flash, we'd be in and rush out with our jerseys full of Brazil nuts. Unfortunately, the Cheshire Lines warehouse received Liverpool's first bomb hit of the war, and many thousands came to look at the bomb crater. However, the bomb had not exploded until it got underground, so there was only a small crater about three feet wide on the road surface. The Lord Mayor, Sir Sidney Jones, came down to see it. He was a small man with a little white moustache, and he spoke to us all. I suppose as kids we were overawed at talking to the Mayor of Liverpool. He reigned in office throughout the war years; normally the Mayor only holds office for one year.

The Cheshire Lines warehouse bombing was just the start of things to come. In 1940 (before the May Blitz), a bomb fell in the Park Street end of the tenements, killing 14 people. This bomb was a shrapnel bomb, which was designed to kill or injure anybody near to the explosion. One poor young woman, Peggy Ashcroft, who was an ambulance driver, was horribly cut into two pieces. Her blood was smeared all across the shelter walls.

I remember Teddy Charnoch sitting on the ground, yelling about his legs. When they tried to pick him up, they found both his legs had been practically severed, but he survived his injuries.

One of our pastimes, after the all-clear siren was sounded, was to collect shrapnel.

Looking back, I also remember well the day war was declared. Eddy and I were in the Isle of Man, having a holiday in Douglas, at a little fisherman's cottage.

It was on a Sunday in September, 1939. My mother decided to stay on the Isle of Man for the duration of the war. However, we only stayed one day, before we returned to Liverpool. The Isle of Man was later used as a detention camp for prisoners of war. The promenade was off limits for the public and there was barbed wire across every little street off Strand Street. The ferries to and from Douglas zig-zagged their way to Liverpool, as there were German U-boats in the Irish Sea. On the point off Crosby, there were man-made structures in the sea, manned with anti-aircraft guns. Bootle suffered badly from bombing, possibly the worst area, outside London, to be bombed in the country, especially in the May blitz of 1941. The whole of Church Street was badly hit and South Castle Street was damaged badly, but the statue in Queen's Square of Queen Victoria remained intact. The Queen Victoria statue was situated at the centre of the site, of the old Liverpool castle, built in the 14th century, and finally cleared the castle in the 18th century.

Liverpool also suffered badly. One poor soul worked as a storeman at the Brunswick Dock for T&J Harrison's. One day his house took a direct bomb hit while he was at work. I believe his whole family was wiped out, with the exception of a young baby who was thrown out of a window and survived. It was said that when Nelson Street (part of China Town) got bombed, they found some Chinese men in a basement of one of the houses. They were all dead and had been sitting around a table gambling. There was still a pile of cash on the table! Another bad explosion occurred when an ammunition train received a direct hit.

Liverpool was the second largest city (after London) to be bombed. It really annoyed us that whenever Liverpool was bombed, the B.B.C. would never mention the city by name, just referring to 'a north-west town'. Other cities such as Coventry, Birmingham, Plymouth or any other, would be acknowledged by name, but we were a 'north-west town'. It became an affront to us not to have a name.

Some of the wardens tended to be over officious in their duties. One of the most common calls at night time was, "PUT THAT BLOODY LIGHT OUT!" These were the wardens, who wore a white tin helmet with a big W on it. These were men who were too old to be enlisted in the forces, or men who were not fit for call up. They worked alongside the police and did a great job on the home front.

The blackout was a necessary nuisance during the war. We had no street lighting, and all transport had a grill on their headlights which had to make the lighting shine down. Even if you lit up a cigarette outside, the warden could jump on you with, "Put that light out!" There is a programme on the television called "Dad's Army" which is near the truth of those far-off days. The Home Guard started off as the Civil Defence Guard. They had no light arms, and trained with brush poles. We were ready to take on the Hun… thank Christ the Germans didn't invade us. Most of the Home Guard had served in the First World War, and these poor buggers had seen war at its worst. They used mobile anti-aircraft guns which ran around the streets. They put the frighteners up you when you didn't expect it and there was a deafening bang right outside your house and everywhere shook.

I must add, there were women doing the same jobs as the men folk. There were many jobs that the women had to do during the war. They drove trams, and thousands worked in factories making armaments, driving cranes, all doing their bit. My mother had to find work in Liverpool as there was no work in the Isle of Man. She found work brushing up at the Cheshire Lines Goods sheds, which was a lousy job and dirty work, scraping the muck out of the rails. Then she got a job working at

R&J Evans Ship Repairers, in the joiners' shop, cleaning up and making the tea, which was a cushy job. The firm was in Caryl Street at the corner of Stanhope Street. The firm opposite was a ship's scaling outfit called Clare's. During the war there was a lot of corruption, this firm was taken to court on a charge of corruption and fraud. The charge was taking government money by fraud. Their books had men on the payroll list who were not working for Clare's. The owner of Clare's committed suicide. Porter's, a scaling outfit, was also heavily fined under the same charge. Porter's is still in existence and are famous for making flags, from the Royal Standard, to flags all over the world.

I remember the church in Cornwallis Street called St Thomas' was bombed. As I worked close by, I saw German prisoners of war clearing the rubble of St Thomas'. We spoke to them and one said he had been on the bombing raid, and now had to clear up the rubble he had caused. We didn't feel any hatred towards these men. I suppose in Germany during the thirties they were indoctrinated by 'Mein Kampf', the Nazi bible. It could have happened anywhere. Germany, like us, was going through a bad depression, and people were desperate for relief. Hitler gave employment to the masses. He built the autobahns, presided over the development and production of the people's car, the Volkswagen, one of the most popular cars ever built.

Unfortunately, Hitler wanted the whole world to accept his doctrine. It is entirely possible that people were blind to what was going on politically in Germany. It might sound naïve, but some of the working class people in Germany may have been unaware of the gravity of the situation and where Hitler was taking them. Given the chance, he would have annihilated a whole race of people. He did, of course, succeed in slaughtering six million Jews and gypsies. Hitler had a great admiration for the British, as although we are a small island nation, we had taken a fifth of the world under our wing in the empire. He really wanted the U.K. to join him and pursue his ideals, but thank God, we thought differently. The U.K. did not take the

Jack Stamper

path of the holocaust, and try to wipe out a whole nation.

Soon afterwards, in early 1940, Eddy and I were evacuated to North Wales. This only lasted about three months and we returned home to experience more bombing. The worst time for incessant bombing was early May 1941. We had eight nights of the Blitz. Liverpool was a target as it was the port where the food convoys were organized. The main control centre was in a deep underground cellar in Old Hall Street.

During the war it was very bad living in the dock area. The bombing got worse and by 1941, it had become really bad. Then the May blitz hit us. We had eight nights of constant bombings. There were two big, communal air raid shelters that served the four blocks of tenements where we lived. We never liked going in the shelter, as it had a foul smell. We decided we'd sleep in our own beds, and sod the danger of the tenements been hit by a bomb.

There was a horrible disaster at an air-raid shelter in the basement of Clint Road School. The school received a direct hit, and as well as the bomb blast, the poor buggers inside also had to suffer the cascade of scalding hot water from the boilers. I believe no one survived and over 200 lost their lives, mostly women and kids.

The firm I would soon be working for, Howson's, was badly damaged when a Brocklebank ship called the *Malakand* was unlucky enough to be hit with incendiary bombs. Unfortunately, the ship was loaded with ammunition. This caused the largest explosion the port ever experienced. Blast forces can play some unusual tricks. The blast travelled across to the west side of Huskisson dock and then returned back to the adjoining dock, Huskisson No. 2, and sank ships there. Huskisson No. 2 was so badly damaged they had to fill it in. Howson's was based opposite the dock, at the corner of Sandhills and Regent Road. One of the ships' plates flew two miles to land on and flattened a small car. The two innocent occupants were killed outright as they drove along Derby Road. This was about the time that my father was called up for the Army. He went out to Egypt with the R.A.S.C. Regiment and didn't come home for four years.

Another victim of the bombings was the Custom House, where we kids from Brunswick Gardens would often meet up. This was a beautiful building; it would have been a grade one listed building today, second in beauty only to Saint George's Hall Building.

Canning Place wrapped around the building, the front of the building was on the dock road. There were large steps leading up into the huge main doors. Massive, round columns held up the magnificent portico. I remember if you came down Park Lane into Canning Place, right opposite were four foot steel posts with chains on. There was an open entrance, where you could walk through the building. It had three archways, which were open to the public. Once inside, if you looked up you would see a massive dome. When you came out the other side, South Castle Street was opposite, with lots of small shops on either side. The basement of the Custom House was used as a large emergency water tank. The walls of the building were four feet thick.

The Custom House had to be pulled down. It was like a part of the city's heart was being ripped out. It was such a beautiful building. I am sure that in these days, they would have saved this building. The worst damage was caused by incendiary bombs, it was badly damaged by fire, but the superstructure was sound. However, in those days, buildings were not listed.

If you carried on walking up South Castle Street, about 100 yards up on the left was Crooked Lane. This was a very interesting lane. Halfway down Crooked Lane, on the right, was Bens Gardens. This was where solicitors had their offices. Bens Gardens was paved with huge stone flags, some eight feet across, from the eighteenth century. I remember they had beautiful gilded gates to the street entrance. Mercer Court was the second turning on the right. Crooked Lane was so named as it twisted and turned, and at each corner there was fixed a barrel of an old cannon. These had been used in the Crimean war, and now stopped carts damaging the corners of the wall. The lane came out at the north side of Canning Place.

During the war years, the dock road going south ended at Horsefall Street. This road led to the Harrington and Herculaneum docks. Most of docks had a wall or large fence around the perimeter, you had to have a pass to enter the dock estate, and every dock entrance had a policeman guarding the dock. At the Herculaneum Dock, if you needed to go north on the overhead railway, you had to come from Grafton Street, then you would use the iron bridge, which took you over the Cheshire Lines Railway, which was quite high. At the end of the bridge, you had to go over another small bridge, which took you on to the platform of the northbound overhead railway. The stairway up to the northbound platform was blocked off.

This system took place at other stations at the north end of the railway, at the Huskisson Dock. Security was very tight on the docks during the war. When the overhead railway first opened, the Herculaneum was the terminus, and at the other end the Alexandra dock was the end of the line. In 1896 they extended the railway to Seaforth sands at the southern end, and then they built the tunnel to the Dingle end.

As I mention, the cast iron bridge had an interesting view of the steam trains speeding from Central Station onwards to Manchester and eastern parts of the country. Some individuals were a bit nervous crossing the bridge, as it was quite a high bridge, and the noise of the steam trains speeding under the bridge was a great sight to see, with the smoke belching up towards the bridge, coming from the engine.

Sailing to Douglas I.O.Man taken 1946
I look like one of the Mafioso

CHAPTER THIRTEEN

The Apprentice Years

I suppose it was luck that got me serving my time as a shipwright.

My mother was cleaning a lady's house in a beautiful mansion in Prince's Park. When our milkman delivered our milk at home, we could get an extra bottle of milk if we needed it. The lady who my mother worked for was always short of milk, so during the morning I would take her a bottle. The lady asked my mother if her son had no job, and indeed I was unemployed at the time.

The lady asked her daughter's father-in-law, a Mr. D.W. Williams, the Managing Director of the Brocklebank Steamship Company, if there were any job openings. I was duly sent for, and went to his huge office in the Cunard Building. He asked me if I wanted to go to sea. Of course I replied yes, but that I wanted to serve my time. He asked me if I wanted to be a carpenter. That sounded fine to me, so he rang the top man at Howson's, a ship repair firm in Sandhills Lane, Bootle. I started the following week. Mr. Williams said that when I had finished my apprenticeship, I would be given a job with the company. However, this didn't work out as Mr. Williams died soon after, so the job as a carpenter on the Brocklebank ships didn't materialize; the company would only employ experienced sea-going carpenters.

When I first started my apprenticeship, I found that there was a hierarchy. The eldest lad was known as the boss lad, and he certainly let you know where you stood. I was the dog's body and it was always, "Fetch me this, fetch me that!" The

Head Foreman Shipwright was Mr. Stackhouse. He was quite a gentleman, he had a moustache and he wore a bowler hat. Unfortunately, he started to lose his mind. I remember him asking me to go to a certain ship, but two minutes later, he gave me a different order. His second-in-command, George Graham, put me right. Poor old Billy Stackhouse had to retire.

There were no facilities to wash your hands on the dock estate, and the hygiene was very poor on the docks. The toilets were not fit for a dog to use. The toilet was simply a 24-inch pipe with holes at equal intervals. There was no privacy. As lads, we used to set light to a piece of paper and send it along the pipe. You could hear the dockers jumping off the toilet. We would have to run away, but we had a good laugh at their expense.

I started my apprenticeship at the beginning of March, 1946. I was apprenticed to two good shipwrights, Joe Cottier and a great old man, Manuel Marutia, of which he got the name 'Charlie'. He was Spanish and despite being 76 years old, he was as agile as a man in his forties. There were plenty of elderly men still working at the trade, as this was still just after the war years, so the younger men were doing military duty.

Charles Howson's was the firm I was apprenticed at. Howson's was under contract to the Cunard shipping fleet, so all of their ships had priority. This was a time when there was plenty of work for all trades. The passenger liners had been carrying troops for the government, but were now being handed back to the relevant shipping companies. Our firm had the *Ascania, Franconia, Samaria, Scythia, Media, Parthia, Assyria, Asia* and many more Cunarders. We also worked on the Brocklebank line, a fleet of freighters that was a subsidiary of the Cunard line.

Working on the big Cunard liners was an experience. There could be hundreds of workers on board one ship. We, the shipwrights, would be taking up the old decking and laying new wooden decking. The timber we used was Columbian Pine.

#4 Hatch

This was beautiful timber, with a truly straight grain. There was much adze work, but this timber was ideal to work with.

The times I liked best, was when we were making either a topmast or a five-ton derrick. There would be four shipwrights and two apprentices, with two saw trestles set up. On the trestles, a huge 16-inch square log would be marked out. The log was then turned into an octagonal shape, most of the work being done with the adze, then a drawknife was used and the job was finally finished with wooden hollow planes. The wood was finished with boiled oil, then the steel gooseneck was fitted. This was the part of the derrick that swivelled, allowing the derrick to move left or right. There were three steel rings, which were heated up and driven over the gooseneck. The rings were then cooled down with buckets of cold water, so that they contracted and tightened over the gooseneck, the derrick then was tested at the ship, and we always had an audience watching us. Sometimes, if there was a fault in the timber, the derrick would snap. Then there would be plenty of cock (waste) wood to be had, and I used to take a sack full home to my grandma's to fuel the fire. We would have to start over again and make a new derrick. This was quite rare event, when a derrick snapped under the test.

As shipwrights we made many wooden hatch-boards, as ships then had steel beams across the hatch openings, the wooden hatch-boards were placed on the steel beams, this system had been used for hundreds of years. Today the hatches have been modernised with steel covers, but most ships carry containers now, which allows the loading and unloading to be speeded up. Years ago ships being loaded would take up to three weeks to stow cargo by manpower. Containerisation would take two to three days to load a ship today.

Jack Stamper

CHAPTER FOURTEEN

The Liverpool Overhead Railway

The Liverpool Overhead Railway (L.O.R.) ran along the dock road until its demise in 1956. It was privately run, and it only ran for 63 years. The trains started at Herculaneum Dock and ran as far as Seaforth Sands.

By 1896, they extended by tunnelling to the Dingle and the line was extended to Seaforth L.M.S. The railway served every dock, and covered seven miles in all. If you crossed the platform at Seaforth L.M.S., you could catch the train to Southport. During the Aintree race week, the L.O.R. ran to Aintree railway station.

By kind permission of D.W Norton

Note the cranes in the background, the Huskisson dock, also a Blue star boats funnel. The buildings on the right of the picture are Howson's.

The L.O.R. cost £3,466,000 to build; in today's money, it would be £331,000,000. The concept was a brilliant idea, it was designed by Sir Douglas Fox and James Henry Greathead in 1888, and opened by the Marquis of Salisbury in 1893, but the design was poor. It was the first electrified overhead railway in the world, and it also had the first electric signals. New York has an older overhead railway and after more than 125 years, it is still going strong. The New York railway's open track design was a better design, as the elements went straight through it, and it is a higher structure. The steam engines (Bell engines, because they had a bell in the front of the engine, to give a warning) would travel below the overhead railway, and so pumped steam up to the underside of the structure. The weather came in from both sides, both these factors played havoc with the arch supports, which corroded. There were supposed to be run-offs (gullies), but these were always blocked. They never cleared them, so rainwater remained in the gullies. No wonder it was called 'the Dockers' umbrella', it did keep the rain off you! The end of the L.O.R. was nigh as the council started to put buses along the dock road. This took customers away from the L.O.R.; it was losing the battle to keep going,

The L.O.R employed youngsters straight out of school, to man the stations, as they couldn't afford to pay adults. The lack of shipping trade in the south of the city also contributed to its demise. Being a private company, it finally had to close in 1956. I remember a time when I was a cheeky apprentice shipwright going to work, as usual I got on the Overhead at the Dingle. 7d workers were returning to the Huskisson dock and sat in my seat (wooden seats). This was a time when everybody smoked, but one of the carriages was a non-smoker. I would drop the window down, this would cause an uproar. It was "Put that bloody window back up", I would say "Put your ciggy out and I will, this is a non-smoker". I was called a cheeky get, but I got my way.

Towards the end of the fifties, the south end docks closed. There were no more freight shipping companies. Harrison's, Elder Dempster's, Booker's, African Oil, Elder Fifes and many more shipping companies moved away. The remaining shipping prior to the seventies went to the north end docks, in the advent of containerisation, the port with the new added docks at Seaforth.

The port of Liverpool handles twice the tonnage today than in its early heyday. This is mainly because of very much larger cargo ships. Containerization has speeded up loading, as the large containers are packed at factories around the country. This sounds like progress, but unfortunately it has brought unemployment to over 19,000 dockers. Now there are about 350 dockers employed to handle the containers. It must be mentioned that also 20,000 ship-repairers jobs also went to the wall. During this period, the dockers went on strike against containerisation. They picketed the dock entrance gates for over two years, but despite all their endeavours, the T&G union brought it to an end, and most of the men never worked again.

CHAPTER FIFTEEN

Dock Road - Our Playground

At the Custom House we sat on the top steps, watching the wagons carrying sugar, peanuts, apples and anything else you could think of to eat. Wearing a jersey was handy, as if you had a penknife to slice open up a sack of sugar, or peanuts, it was surprising how much you could carry by holding your jersey out.

Opposite the Custom House was the overhead station, which bore the same name, although later the name was changed to Canning Dock. Carrie's was a little kiosk under the stairs that led up to the station. You could buy tea for 1d, or 2d for a larger cup, toast for 1d, or a bacon buttie for 5d. As kids, we thought Carrie was a good looker. Usually, the dockers would give you some of their carry out too. They were the salt of the earth, good men; always ready for a laugh, happy-go-lucky men.

If you could manage to skip onto a steam lorry, the man who stoked the fire would throw lumps of coal at you. Steam wagons were used during the war years. Some of them had been taken from the scrapheap, but they were salvaged and put to use. Most of the wagons were made by Sentinels, they had a good turn of speed, and could do 40m.p.h

A sad tragedy happened to one of our mates, Buller Williams. He was on the wagon and tried to jump onto the trailer. However, he missed his footing and fell between the wagon and trailer. The wheels went over him and he was crushed. We sat him against the wall and stood around him, not knowing what to do. The ambulance took over half hour to come, and by then it was too late. Buller died shortly after that. We were shocked, but it didn't stop us jumping on the backs of the wagons. This tragedy happened outside the Severn Steps pub, at the bottom of Northumberland Street. Alas, the Severn Steps pub is no more; it's an office block now.

Northumberland Street was a long street running from the dock road (Sefton Street) to Windsor Street. At the dock road end there was the huge Cheshire Lines warehouse. The carters went into the yard to unhitch their carts. They then brought the horses up Northumberland Street to the stables in Mann Street. At this time, most of the carting was still done by horsepower, and the dock road was full of good honest horse manure. It must be said the carthorses did sterling work during the war years. The dock road and most roads were paved with granite sets; roads would last forever, but it could be a treacherous surface when wet. I have always believed that there should be something to commemorate the work-horses during the war.

The Seven Steps pub was the last pub on the dock road going south. The landlady, a Mrs. Parker, did a roaring trade as the pub was always packed. Going further to the south, after Park Street, was Horsefall Street. This street was a road bridge that went up over the Cheshire Lines railway to join Caryl Street. Later, the Horsefall Street Bridge was taken away, leaving the remains of two narrow streets with inclines, one facing north and one facing south. You can still see a horse trough at the apex of Horsefall Street and the dock road. Along the dock road there were a number of fresh water stands for the horses.

There was also a footbridge that went over the Cheshire Lines. This linked up with the Herculaneum Overhead Station, and was commonly known as the 'Iron Bridge'. If you went south of the bridge to Grafton Street, you could get a panoramic view of the four dry docks and coal berth, and the oil terminal adjacent to the coal berth. The steam trains used to speed under the bridge on their way to Manchester and eastwards, belching

#4 Hatch

their smoke upwards towards you. The Herculaneum Dock coal berth had two huge cranes that lifted the coal trucks off the railway lines and tipped the coal into a coaster. Opposite the coal berth was an oil tanker berth for small tankers, and further over were four dry docks.

It was some time later, in 1963, that the Herculaneum Dock was finally put out of action. Along with three other shipwrights, I secured the dock gates to the river entrance with 12x12x30 foot long balks of timber. These props or 'shores' were temporarily fixed to dock gates and the quay wall. They were finally concreted to the opening entrance to the river. Up until then, the Dock Board had a river quayside store with beacons and light ships dotted along the wall while they were being overhauled. The small stage that we worked on, while we were closing the river entrance was on the river side, this being 1963. There were large pieces of ice floating down the river, this was during the coldest winter for over 100 years.

The Herculaneum docks were eventually completely filled in. Now, there are offices, flats and a sports gym there. I remember some years before it closed, I dry docked the old *Eaglet*, a nineteenth century sloop. She was a R.N.V.R. training ship and was falling to pieces. Her sister-ship, the *Eagle*, was also in a bad way, and was berthed in the Salthouse Dock. Both ships had to be scrapped, in the dry-dock.

I remember when we were apprentices in 1946, three of us decided to join the R.N.V.R at the *Eaglet*. After about four weeks, the Chief Petty Officer told us we could not be Petty Officers, as we were not yet nineteen and a half. We didn't like this, so we 'swallowed the anchor', the Navy term for resigning. I think we just wanted to be Saturday night sailors to show off to the girls at the Grafton Dance Hall.

In 1946 there was a tragedy taking place on the river opposite Cammel Lairds, a ship called the S.S *Stormont* had a collision with the *Empire Brent* (formerly the *Leticia*) in which she was holed, beneath the water line. The *Stormont* was carrying cattle and horses from Dublin, but the ship could not reach her berth, as she was sinking. They had to send for the R.S.P.C.A authorities to slaughter the livestock. From where we were, we could hear the noise of the humane killer gun, shooting the animals, the dead animals were put in the river, and taken to where we were standing, alongside the high wall of the Albert Dock at the riverside. The cows were stacked one and top of the other, they were all blown up with water and finally wagons had to take them away.

Liverpool has lost some beautiful buildings from those years. Some of them would have been listed buildings today. As I mentioned before, one of the best was the Cheshire Lines Goods warehouse, which is now a Renault car sales depot, at the bottom of Park Street.

The high perimeter wall of the Prince's Dock rose above the dock road. A large tablet was set in the wall, (still there today) stating 'Waterloo Dock, 1848', the date when it was erected. A lot of the construction was done by French prisoners of war, during Napoleonic times.

The building I really must not forget is the famous Goree Piazzas, which ran between James Street and Water Street along the dock road north to south. In the building were companies such as A.B Dalzell's, which made scientific instruments for ships, ships' clocks, and compasses. There was also Nicholsons' sail makers and many more small outlets, and Petties café. At each end of the building was a pub, the pub at the north-end was a well known pub called 'Tom Halls.'

The City Council demolished the Goree Piazzas in the 1960s. I call it legalized vandalism. The building had been erected in the middle to the end of the eighteenth century. The name Gooree was taken from a place in Sierra Leone, West Africa, where many of the slaves came from.

The building was not in the way, as it stood in the centre of the dock road and traffic passed on either side. People said that the ringbolts in the walls were to tie the black slaves to, but I know that this is untrue. The rings were used to lower barrels and other materials into the cellars.

Sunset looking northwards, near the Albert Dock

It is common knowledge that the movement of slaves was a 'triangular movement'. This term described how the slaves were taken from the African coast and shipped like animals to the West Indies or southern states of America. The ships were then loaded with sugar, cotton, rum and other goods bound for the United Kingdom, the ships returned to Africa to pick up more slaves. Many thousands of slaves perished at sea and were dumped over the side of the ships, like jetsam.

Liverpool was the last port to practise this evil trade. You can say that on the backs of the slaves, Liverpool flourished as a port and city in the early twentieth centuries. Liverpool was the second city of the empire. You can see evidence of this in the rich people's large park houses, which are still standing there today.

The Spanish company De Larrinaga's was the oldest foreign company sailing out of Liverpool. The management built their houses in the southern end of the city, around the south's fine parks. In William Roscoe's words, "Parks are the lungs of a city". The land was owned by the council for the well-being of the citizens of Liverpool, where they could take their leisure.

I remember clearly as a young apprentice going to Petties coke room for breakfast in the Goree Piazzas. The café had sawdust on the floor, so you could not see the dirt. It was a cheap meal; 4d for a bacon sandwich, 2d for a cup of tea. In this eating den if you had chips and peas and asked for utensils, the reply was, "Got fingers, haven't ye?" We'd throw the plates to the back of counter, saying, "You eat them, then!" The nice girl, who looked like butter wouldn't melt in her mouth, told us to fuck off. It was hilarious. The other apprentices and I worked close by, regulating the Canning dry dock for a dredger. This was a back breaking job moving elm dock blocks 12 x 12 x 4 feet long, maybe 60 or more to be fastened to the centre line castings. This is were the ship would sit. The blocks would have to be retained after the ship is finished, in these small dry docks, the individual firms had to use your own blocks.

There was another coke room, called Eboe's café, situated in the centre of the Harland & Wolf ship repairers on the dock road in Bootle. It sold lovely cream custards, and on a Thursday, there was boiled bacon and cabbage with boiled potatoes.

I remember we were at the coke room in the Clarence Dock one day, waiting for it to open. At lunchtime, they opened at 11.30am. A man who worked with us, a chargehand shipwright, tried to touch the girl's bum as she came to open the cafe. She spun round and whacked him across the face with a wet dishcloth. "You dirty bastard!" she exclaimed, and we egged her on as she dealt out justice the only way she knew. Bert got his reward for messing around.

There were also YMCA coke rooms. These were the cleanest

canteens on the docks. They were so clean; you could eat off the floor. However, the canteen at the Queen's Dock was inside a shed. We knew it as the rat house. It was a scruffy hole, where pieces of the rotting roof used to fall into your dinner. Once you found this out, you never went there again. Today, most of these eating-places would be closed down under the Health and Safety Acts.

The term coke room is derived from the early part of the 20th century, when the dockworkers started work very early. The tearooms would be open and sold a mixture of rum and cocoa, known as coke. This was a warm drink in the winter for the dock workers. It is now no longer available.

CHAPTER SIXTEEN

Young Lad's Games

We made steering-carts out of old planks of wood, two axles, four pram wheels and some rope. Outside the tenements in Northumberland Street, the pavement sloped down steeply to Caryl Street, where we built a ramp. We sped downhill and hit the ramp, trying to see who could launch themselves the furthest. We finished up with some fine scrapes on our knees, arms and everywhere, but it was great fun.

Utny (leapfrog) was another great game. The idea was to toss up, and then whoever lost had to bend over. For the next part, you always picked Charlie Dybell. He was always selected, as he was the best athlete. The person picked had to leap from the edge of the kerb, over to the opposite kerb, over the lad who was bent over. Charlie would sail straight over the bent-over lad; only Charlie could do it. He would take a long run and literally dive over the man who was bent over. He never injured himself!

Our Eddy was a right entrepreneur. To make some money, he would find old timber from some bombed building. He would then take the axe from the house, go to Caryl Street and chop up the wood to sell as firewood. He organized some of the younger kids to carry the bundles of firewood to the various houses in the tenements. My mother would know where he was, from the sound of the axe clinking on the stones in Caryl Street.

I remember there was a time when a gang of us went to Oglet near Hale village, to scrump apples from an orchard. It was like a pantomime. As we emerged from the orchard, we found that the whole of Hale village had been alerted to our crime. The chase was on. From the villagers' reaction, you would have thought that the Germans had landed!

One policeman and the villagers chased us across the fields. Eight of us got caught. Our Eddy ran towards Halewood lighthouse, chased by someone from the village. Our kid stopped, and there was a stand off. As he was the only one on the chase, I think the chaser didn't like the odds. Since it was one on to one, he backed off.

One lad, 'Ucker' Johnson, was craftier than the rest of us. He stayed in the orchard while we were being chased all over the place. While we were being hunted down, he trotted out of the orchard and went home with all his apples.

The policeman took our names and shortly afterwards, we were summoned to appear at Widnes Magistrates Court. We were fined 7/6 pence, although there were too many of us to get in the dock. The lady who owned the orchard was most upset because of the trouble it caused. She would have liked us not to be prosecuted. As well as the apples, Oglet was also a good place to pick bunches of daffodils to take home. One of the lads who got caught was Dave Jameson, who was to be called up to join the navy the day of the court hearing. He never went to court, and was excused.

I remember during an air raid, Billy Mac came into the shelter. Someone asked him, "I thought you were called up for the Army, Bill?" to which Billy replied that he didn't like the Army. That was his answer. The next day, the military police took him away, back to the Army where he would serve 5 years before his demob.

Billy was a character who made us laugh. One of the many warehouses that was bombed in Caryl Street was the L.N.E.R. warehouse. It caught fire and the remains smouldered for three years. There was a terrible stench as it had contained animal food and copra, which causes a terrible smell.

Heinz's warehouse also was bombed, we ate tinned soup for weeks. You could be shot for looting, but my mother spotted a special policeman filling his respirator bag with tins of fruit. He nearly had a heart attack when he realized he was being watched, and pleaded with my mother not to tell anybody. Looting was a very serious offence during the war.

The Overhead Railway was hit by bombs three times, at the Gladstone Dock, Huskisson Dock and James Street, but they had it running again within weeks. There were lots of coke rooms on the dock road, such as Stan Water's, Cottral's, Petties, McConnel's, the YMCA and many more. Tea cost 1p for a small cup or 3d for a large cup and a dinner comprising of watery potatoes or chips with fish or pie would cost 10 pence. Watery soup was 3d and the sweet, either steam pudding or rice, would cost 3d. There was also a deposit of 2/- for your cup, knife, fork and spoon. I was living with my grandma, who was always wondering where her knives and forks went missing to. Sometimes we worked on a Cunard passenger ship, where you could always find cutlery lying around somewhere.

There was a docker's canteen at the bottom of Bankfield Street and the dock road. In the cellar of The Dominion pub (the pub still exists), the tea urn was unbelievable. The man filled a lady's stocking with dry tea tied at the leg end, and hung it inside the urn. In this way, he made the first tea bag. The cups were literally dipped into the urn to be filled. It wasn't very clean, but it was a quick way to dish out tea.

There were some characters on the dock estate. One was a big, burly man, who would have concrete slabs placed on his chest. Anybody who could swing a sledgehammer was allowed to swing at the slab, which would break into two pieces. He then passed his cap around, hoping to get a few bob. He trusted anyone to use the hammer. One day someone missed the slab and hit his arm; his arm broke. This happened near to Bootle Hospital, he didn't think it was a problem. He simply had a cast put on, then came straight back and carried on with his show.

Two other men were escapologists. One would tie a sack over his head with chains, and roll around in the mud trying to get the chains off. When he got out, he would be in a right state! This was our free entertainment.

Another man was a tipster, who'd always wear riding breeches and would say anything for a few bob. His line would be something like, "I was talking to Sir Gordon Richards this morning, he gave me two certainties running in 2.30 race, and one in the 3.30!" Nobody believed him.

There was a policeman at every dock gate to stop pilfering from the docks. Some of these policemen were right bastards. I saw a carter with a team of horses coming through the gate one day. The cart had big packing cases on it. The copper inspected the load and spotted a couple of pieces of timber (used as skids) that were under the cases. He made the man take the loaded cart back to the shed, unload it and remove the skids. The carter called the copper every name under the sun.

Some of the policemen had nicknames, like 'One-a-day'. I was coming out of the Huskisson Dock one day with a shipwright named Teddy McKay, who always rode a bike. Tea was still rationed, Ted had his saddle bag stuffed full of tea. The copper stopped him, asking, "What have got in the saddle bag?" Ted had a naturally miserable face and replied sarcastically, "Me bloody dinner," continuing, "Do you want to see what's in the bloody sandwiches?" The copper had had enough, and told us to beat it and not be so bloody cheeky. Now, that's what I call bluff!

I remember the great Billy McBride. We were working on a Yankee boat at Gladstone Dock and Mac found a big tin of butter down the hatch. I asked how he was going to get that out of the gate. "Watch me!" he said, and flattened the tin to about two inches thick. He then shoved it up his shirt and walked out the gate, no problem. The next day he told me his wife had had to scrape the butter off his belly!

The Russian Kruzenstern one of the largest sailing ships in the world, visiting Liverpool during the Tall Ships visit, 2005

There was a time while I was sailing as a carpenter in the *Bothnia*, when we were in Glasgow discharging cargo. I was talking to the ship's Watchman, he told me the tale of the whiskey episode. He was guarding the whiskey cases down in the ships hold, but before he knew it, the Glasgow dockers had stacked the cases in such a way that he was walled in with cases. As he couldn't get out, they helped themselves to the whiskey. While I was in Glasgow, I was introduced to the Harrison Line shore skipper, who was the skipper of the famous ship the *Politician*, which was featured in the film *Whiskey Galore*. This was the time of the dock strike of 1954, where we had to spend some weeks up in Glasgow.

I went ashore one night with the shore-gang in Glasgow to some local pub. They all drank a strange concoction of half of bitter and a glass of "Glava" (a strong liquor) and after a session of drinking this stuff, you were blown over. While having a drink during the lunch hour in the pub along side the docks,

#4 Hatch

I noticed all the dockers were drinking a half and half (half of bitter and a glass of whiskey); this was their normal drink.

The Langton Dry-Dock Pumping station, one of the finest pieces of brickwork in the North-West; there is a preservation order on it. Thos is a place were, as shipwrights, we would in the winter get a warm in the boiler room, during a dry-docking of a ship.
Built in the mid-19th century.

CHAPTER SEVENTEEN

My Life on the Docks

After the war there was plenty of work to be done. All ships had to have a general overhaul. The type of work which was related to my trade, being a shipwright, meant that the wooden decking, wooden handrails, hatch boards, work below in the hatches would be in a bad state of repair, and most of it had to be replaced. After the wooden decking was laid, the new decking had to be caulked with oakum. Oakum is a raw rope fibre, which was treated with Stockholm tar. Firstly, you spun your oakum, (teasing it) by having to use a piece of canvas on your knee, where you rolled it across your knee, then rolling it into a ball. After the oakum was caulked in the deck planks, it was ('paying up time'). A big ladle, shaped like a spoon, was used to pour melted Bitumen tar between the planks. One man was given the job who would be a scaler, which was to scrape the cold pitch off the deck with a sharpened three-cornered, long-handled scraper. This was dirty work, the deck was brushed clean. The deck was then finally finished with a deck planer.

I remember the dock board tender the *Ranger*. She had been in commission for 70 years and she had a wooden hull. Her decks were made of teak, and after laying the deck and caulking it, the seams of the decking were filled with white marine glue. After the glue was scraped off the planks, the decking looked a treat, with white lines against the teak wood. The *Ranger* had also had teak handrails, and the hull was made of oak.

Howson's also had a contract with the Booker Line. This company sailed to British Guiana. One of their ships, the *Arakaka*, was a small cargo and passenger ship. The carpenter of the ship told me that at sea, they would put up a sail on the foremast to gain another knot of speed. Another ship they had was the *Amakura*. Their main import was Greenheart logs, a very heavy and dense timber that was ideal for underwater work, for example dock gates.

One day, the *Amakura* came in to discharge a consignment of timber when the ship had a problem with one of the logs. The dockers could not retrieve it from the hold, as it was too long to bring it out of the hold. Try as they might there was nothing they could do. They had to leave the log in the ship until she returned from her next trip, then they took one of the plates off the side of the hull, to remove the log.

I remember one time, an apprentice Lennie Williams and I were working overtime at the *Robert L. Holt* at the Brunswick Dock. After we finished work, we decided to make our way north. As we were passing the Dukes Dock, we saw an old lifeboat. Being lads, we decided to go for a row. It was getting dark and as we got further away from the quay, the boat started to take on water. We just about made it to the steps, before it sank.

We had other work to do, such as stabilizing cargo in the ships, which was known as 'chocking' (or 'tomming') off. I remember being sent to a Yankee ship named the *Seaforth* in the Langton Dock. This ship had five hatches full of large khaki coloured boxes. We realised these were coffins that contained U.S. servicemen killed in action. During the war, there must have been thousands of them loaded onto ships to be taken back to the States, for reburial at home.

To work alongside Liverpool dockers is an experience not to be forgotten. Their humour is natural. As they were loading these coffins, the hatch boss shouted down to the men, "You could squeeze a couple more in the wings of the hatch, they won't feel the pinch!"

One time another Yankee ship, the S.S. *Ruth Lykes*, had been up to Glasgow and was loaded with cases of whiskey in the deep tanks. The ship came to Liverpool to pick up a load of cars for America. (Britain was actually exporting cars in the fifties.) As the dockers were loading the cars, we were working alongside them, chocking the cars off to prevent them from moving about at sea. The Chief Officer, knowing that the dockers would be after the whiskey, had a car placed over the manhole lid of the deep tank, where the whiskey was stored. However, the dockers were crafty. One of the dockers, who must have been a snake, crawled under the car, undid the bolts and slithered down into the hold. He then passed the whiskey up to his mates.

We were unaware of what was going on, until we noticed that the dockers were getting a little inebriated. After a while, they couldn't stand up and had to send down a cargo net to lift them up out of the hold. The American Chief Officer was dumbfounded, but he had to smile. All he said was, "The cheeky bastards!"

Working on the docks could be very dangerous. I remember a time I was sent to the west Langton Dock to give two shipwrights a hand on a big Yankee freighter called the *Sea Perch*. As she was a light ship with no cargo aboard, she was high out of the water. We were working on the ship's lifeboats.

I was sent to the Howson's yard to get some materials for the job, and I had my lunch at the yard. I came back at 1.00pm to the ship, to find the police and ambulances there. To my horror, I found out that my two mates had removed the gripes that secured the lifeboats from tipping over. One of them had then accidentally knocked the release hook, which was the only thing holding the 30 foot steel lifeboat onto the ship. Unfortunately, the boat tipped and fell, and landed on the deck of another ship, the *Colorado Springs Victory,* that was berthed alongside. I will never forget the sight. Poor Bert Foster was cut in two and Paddy Sullivan was so badly injured, he never worked again. The boat must have fallen 40 feet. I count myself very lucky that I was somewhere else at the time. Their names Foster and Sullivan sound like a comedy duo, but I am not laughing.

There were many accidents on the docks, of which many were fatal. I had my share of accidents. One day while my mate and I were carrying hatch-boards, across the hatch, I fell down the hatch, but I was lucky, I managed to fall on my feet. Being young, I could take the knocks. There was another time, when we were working on the Cunard liner the *Franconia*. She had been a troopship during the war. I remember on the foremast, as it was hollow, you had to go up inside the mast to get to the crow's nest, but some bugger had locked the exit door. I had to climb down the rigging, outside the mast to get down, but luckily I was not scared of heights.

After the war ended, all the large passenger liners were to be returned to their owners, as they had been under the government contract to be used as troopships.

The Board of Trade decided to test all the lifeboats. This would be 1946 at the Gladstone Dock. The ship was the *Samaria*, We lowered the lifeboats into the water, as the lifeboats were never put to use, and not maintained properly they nearly all sank. There would have been a great loss of life if the ship had been torpedoed; the boats were bloody useless. The lifeboats were moved in to the north western Gladstone Dock shed to be repaired. This was a draughty place to work in, but over a period of time, we practically rebuilt the lifeboats.

There were some characters worked for Howson's, especially Billy McBride. He was a tall, scrawny man of 75 years. He was a brilliant all rounder. He had sung at the Bootle Town Hall, and he was good at table tennis. The big Cunard ships all had table tennis facilities for the passengers to use, so while they were being overhauled, we used them. Billy wore clogs and he did all the loft jobs. This meant, if the mast head light needed to come down, Billy would go up for it. He was also the best adze man I ever saw. I would say Billy was young at heart. He liked to be among the lads. Nobody could use the adze like Billy. The tool called the adze was used for shaping timber, and was developed by the Egyptians thousands of years ago.

Alf Acton was also a good shipwright, and he was the yardman, also the top boat-builder. He built the 'Jolly Roger' model boat in Sefton Park in the 1920s, which alas is no more. Nearly all these older men had seen active service in the First World War, and some even in the Boer War.

Another man with whom I worked was Bob Smith. He told me of his experiences when he was the Commodore Carpenter of the Cunard fleet. He sailed as carpenter for 20 years in the old *Mauritania* until she was scrapped in 1936. Shortly after this, he retired from the sea and worked for Howson's. When the war started in 1939 Bob was in his sixties. He was asked by Cunard if he would like to sail with the *Lancastria* to pick up the troops from Dunkirk. The *Lancastria* was the sister ship to the *Ascania*. There were 14,000-ton passenger ships, on the North American run.

During the retreat from Dunkirk, we were no match for the enemy. When they got down there, the *Lancastria* picked up 5,000 troops.

As the *Lancastria* was just about to set sail, a German bomber got lucky, one of his bombs went down the ship's funnel. She blew up the ship's boilers, and sank within minutes. This tragedy was the worst loss of life at sea ever recorded; over 4,000 lives were taken. Bob had no time to pick up his life jacket before he had to jump into the oil-infested sea. When he came to the surface, the sea was covered in three inches of oil. Bob struggled to stay at the surface, but after a short time he was in such difficulty that he decided to end it all, and visit Davy Jones' locker. For some reason, even with all the carnage raging all around him, he finally decided to have a go to try and save himself, when he came to the surface and floated around in the grunge. Eventually, he was picked up by a little fishing boat, although by then he looked so bad, they thought he was dead. Bob told me up till then, he was quite a fit man, but the *Lancastria* episode badly affected his lungs.

Another character was Harold Clegg. Poor Harold, he was a penny short of a shilling. He lived on his own and didn't look after himself. His workmate said once that Harold couldn't get to work this morning as he had a hard on, and couldn't get his pants on. Harold could play the piano, and the apprentices would stand round the piano in the music room, on the ship, singing, "Life is like a lemon, squeeze it while you can, you're a long, long, time dead!" I think Harold composed it himself. He was a harmless soul, but didn't like soap and water.

I was working one time at the Clarence dry dock when I heard a carter, shouting, 'Who has taken my bloody horse?' He finally spotted the horse at the bottom of the dry dock. The horse looked none the worse, and was still munching on his proven bag. Some nutters had taken the horse out of the shafts, put a wide bellyband on it and lowered it into the dry dock.

I remember working at this same graving dock on a coaster. The boilermakers were working in the double bottoms, which were 2ft 6in spaces between the ship's bottom and the hatch bottom. Plates known as intercostals (a steel plate which spanned the gap between the ship's bottom and hatch bottom), the plates had mansize holes which you had to climb through, when you worked down there. These were tanks, which held either fresh water or ballast. One day, the boilermaker had left his burning gear in the double bottom, but forgot to close the valve tight on the acetylene burning gear, the gas seeped out. Two ship's scalers went into the tank, using tallow candles to light their way, as there was no electricity on the ship. As they approached the work area, there was an almighty explosion.

The fire brigade had to bring the two poor, unfortunate men out in sacks. There was not much left of them and the whole tank top was blown open.

There were many horrible accidents happening on the docks and shipyards; there was no Health and Safety at Work Act in the forties. The worst accident I saw was in Cammell Lairds, when they were testing the high hammerhead crane. They had lifted these huge, concrete slabs halfway up when the sling holding the weights snapped and the slabs dropped, literally flattening the three men. The crane driver had to be taken to the hospital with shock, and he never drove a crane again.

I could tell of many more accidents. There was a time, when the tugboat *Applegarth* was assisting two other tugs to bring in a cargo boat into the Birkenhead entrance. The tug's rubber or chaffing bar caught the ship's plate, but as the cargo boat was moving, it tilted the tug, so that it turned the *Applegarth* over. She sank in seconds and three of the crew were lost. The tug had to be brought to the surface quickly, as she was blocking the entrance to the Birkenhead Docks.

There was a time I remember when I was working at the Vittoria dock in Birkenhead, at a Brocklebank boat named the *Mahsud*. As I was passing the China berth quay, everyone was looking down at the water. Some poor bugger was laying face down in the water. What had happened to this poor unfortunate was that the young engineers played a prank. They had put the rudder in his bunk, he returned to the boat deck to replace the rudder he slipped and fell 40 feet down on to the quay and fell into the water. He had been lodged under the bilge keel, and he surfaced when the ship was moved. The ship's crew had thought he was ashore somewhere; he had been stuck under the bilge keel for 3 weeks.

There was plenty of work on the shipping repair side in the early years after the war, but the work was starting to decline during the last years of the fifties. There had been a time when all the docks were full of ships. At the Gladstone Dock, there were United States Lines, the Canadian Pacific with their liners the 'Empress' boats, the large freighters, like those of the Blue

Funnel Line, Federal Line fridge boats and sometimes the Whaling factory ships. The old White Star ships such as the *Britannic* and *Georgic* were still painted in the old White Star colours, buff and black. These ships were now under the Cunard flag.

The *Georgic* was badly bombed in West Africa. You could see the thick hull plates buckled from the fires, but she was overhauled, and saved, and put back in service.

It was a great sight to see the crews of these liners joining the ship's deck hands when they were ready to sail. The catering department had the largest crews, with chefs, cooks, waiters.

Everyone relied on overtime, which supplemented your wages. If you were sent to a Yankee boat (United States Lines) there was always overtime tomming off cargo. Sometimes, if you struck lucky, you could get to work all night. I remember being sent to a Brocklebank boat in the Huskisson dock called the *Mahsirah*. She had brought grain from Canada. In the hold were large baulks of timber, heavy plywood, used for division boards. We started work late afternoon Thursday and worked non-stop until Saturday noon. It took us a week to get over it; we were knackered.

In those days we actually exported British cars to the States. In the late forties and early fifties, there was a spate of ships catching fire in the docks. It was alleged that it was sabotage. One of biggest fires was on the *Empress of Canada*, in the Gladstone Dock.

She went up in flames, while she was getting a refit. There were many workers on the ship at the time, but thankfully no one was injured. It was a terrible sight as the ship keeled over towards the quayside, with her two large funnels smashed on the quay, but I don't think it was sabotage. Her original name was the *Duchess of Bedford*, and her sister ship was the *Duchess of Richmond*, then renamed the *Empress of France* when both ships were taken over by the Canadian Pacific line. They were beautiful liners, both twin funnellers.

The *Empress of Canada* had to be raised from the Gladstone Dock. Her funnels were smashed on the quay, but we managed to take our toolboxes off the ship before the blaze took hold. Raising the ship was a difficult job that required some thought, as she was lying on her side. It was quite a salvaging feat. They had to erect 3 massive winches on the opposite quay, and fasten huge tripods to the side of the hull. The winch cable ran across the dock over the tripods, to the ship's side under the water. While a number of water pumps worked to pump water out of the ship, they then heaved the 26,000 ton ship upright. She had to be scrapped.

However, there were further incidents. One ship I remember was the *Empire Waverly*. This was a captured German passenger cargo ship of about 14,000 tons. The ship mysteriously caught fire. They put it down to sabotage but there was never any evidence shown of what caused the fire. She also had to be scrapped.

The Gladstone Dock being the largest dock in the port, all the larger vessels berthed there.

The old White Star company who owned the *Titanic* and *Majestic* ect, the White Star names all ended in '-ic',

The Cunard line, who took over the White Star fleet, all ended in '-ia' except the Queens. Their colours were red and black funnels.

Today's passenger ships are far larger, but the ships at that period had much nicer lines. There was more pride in designing ships. I remember seeing the big Cunard vessels berthed at the Gladstone Basin waiting to go through the locks to enter the river. The liners would head down the river to the Prince's Landing Stage. This is where the passenger ships took on the passengers, maybe bound for New York or other faraway ports.

The River Mersey was always full of ships. I use to like joining the ship at Gladstone Dock to give the ship's carpenter a hand to fasten down the hatches. We'd disembark at the landing stage.

#4 Hatch

There were times when the *Flying Breeze* (a tender) would take us out into the river to go aboard the ship. She was a huge tug boat, which was built to assist the smaller tugs in nudging the large vessels into the right place. These were happy days, the Mersey was full of ships.

Some cargo boats were very large. I remember the *City of Barcelona* in particular. She had a 180 ton lifting derrick, called the jumbo derrick. She would transport large locomotives all over the world. This kind of cargo was mainly for U.N.R.O., the United Nations Relief Organization.

I worked on the old Mersey Docks and Harbour Board tender the *Ranger*. She had a wooden hull with teak decks. She was still in commission at 70 years old. I also worked on the *Galatia*. She looked like a beautiful yacht and opened the Gladstone Graving Dock in 1923. At that time, this was one of the largest dry docks in the world.

Once, Howson's took on a strange repair job. The boat was called the *Brita Thordon* and was registered in Helsinki, Finland. She had been laid up throughout the war in a London dock. All the deck rivets had been removed. The rivet holes had been replaced with wooden plugs, she was lucky to get up to Liverpool! The ship was known as a logger and her bulwarks were nine feet high to allow more timber to be stored on deck. She was only 2,500 tons. We completed the refurbishments, we made a good job of her.

As I mentioned before in the early fifties, there was a massive fire in the Gladstone Dock shed. Rubber bails caught fire and the avenue was literally a river of rubber. What a mess it must have been to clear up. They took months to clear the rubber.

I remember the lifting of the S.S. *Silvo* from the Langton Dock. The ship had been bombed and sunk during the war. To lift it, they had to call on the *Mammoth* floating crane, the largest floating crane in the world. The crane had a working load of 200 tons.

As the ship had been underwater for some years, she first had to be cut by up acetylene under the water. This was the first time that underwater cutting and welding had been attempted. It was a huge success, but unfortunately they miscalculated the weight of the bow section. As the *Mammoth* crane was slowly lifting the bow section up out of the water and it reached about 20 feet high, there was suddenly an almighty 'ping' as the wire hawsers with a nine inch girth, snapped, the bow dropped back into the water. The crane had been listing from the weight of the bow, and now swung side to side. This part of the job had taken a month's work, and now they had to start again. The weight had been over estimated. They eventually cleared the wreck.

One of the dirtiest jobs we had to do was securing the exported cars going to the States. The ship we worked on was one of the Lykes Lines and had been shipping carbon black on her previous trip. You'd get covered with carbon dust and we never got any extra pay, although we had a job getting the dirt out of our skin.

Our work also often involved lifting heavy weights. Some of the heaviest I experienced were when we had to ram out the castings from the centre line in the graving dock, while a ship was sitting in the blocks. We had to take out maybe five castings. To do this we had to bend over, as the height from the dock to the bottom of the ship was only about 4 feet 6 inches. The tool we used was a 12-handed steel ram, in other words a 12 feet, 6 inches thick long solid steel ram with 12 short lengths of rope attached, twelve men held onto each short rope we then swung it backwards and forwards striking the knob end of the casting. The castings were wedge-shaped, so this would drive the casting out. We had to strike it by swinging the ram in unison, and it took real collective manpower. After we removed the castings, the boilermakers would do their work and when they had finished, we had to put the castings back up again by ramming them back up. Building the pyramids must have been a doddle compared to this backbreaking, wet and dirty work.

Another heavy job involved the ship's cable. The anchor was lowered into the bottom of the dry dock and the anchor cable (chain) was dragged or laid up and down the dock bottom. At every six fathoms along the cable there were shackles. We had to take out the pins of the shackles using a 56lb short-shafted hammer, called a "Monday hammer".

The apprentice pay was rubbish. In your first year, you got paid the paltry sum of 21 shillings a week. This increased by ten shillings each additional year you served your apprenticeship. You were only given 20 shillings a year for tool money. Even in those times, you couldn't buy much with this. This had to cover all your tools, and shipwrights needed a broad range of tools.

As apprentices we always went to Potts' tool shop in Park Lane. The shop had a sign of a big wooden saw hanging outside. Mr. Potts wore a cap and a white apron. He was a large, rotund man, who had a quite severe manner.

As apprentices, we were always up to some devilment. There was a time when the dockers had finished for lunch, so we decided to have a go on their electric bogies. One of the lads got overambitious and steered his bogie too close to the quay. It went into the dock, we did a runner!

I finished my apprenticeship in the beginning of 1951. Things were getting bad for the shipping firms.

If you became unemployed, there was a stand, which meant you had to present yourself at Howson's, or Harland & Wolf, Grayson & Rollo, A&R Brown's or Crichton's yard at seven thirty if you wanted to work. It was like a cattle market; in other words, if your face fitted you got a start, maybe for a couple of days work. You always got laid off just before the bank holidays, so they didn't have to pay you for the bank holidays.

There were times when there was no work at all. Then you went on the pool, which meant that you reported to the Regent Road dole office every day, including Saturday mornings, to go on the register for casual work on dry-docking or undocking ships. You were paid a whole day's labour for a docking (securing a ship in the Dry-dock), or half a day for an un-docking (taking the ship out of the Dry-dock). This meant at the end of the week, we'd have to travel to each firm to get wages, up and down the length of docks.

I remember one time we were ordered to a job at the Langton Dock at 4am. You had to make your own way to the dock, since there were no public services running. I went on my bicycle. The job was to regulate the dock and get all the shores (wooden props) ready. The boss then told us that the ship we were supposed to dry-dock did not make the tide, so the job was cancelled. We were told to report back to the dole that morning, and we received 2 hours attendance pay. This meant that we lost our dole money for that day. In essence, this also meant it cost us money to go to work, as the 2 hours pay was less than a day's dole money. I got the union delegate down to inform him what was going on and the employers agreed to pay us at least a guaranteed minimum of half day's pay for each job.

I remember when I was a young apprentice; the boss gave orders to report to the Canada dry dock at an unearthly hour in the morning. Again, you had to make your own way there. This was in the winter of 1947, where the snow was four feet deep in places. It was the worst winter for snow ever recorded. At that time I lived in the Lodge Lane area. I got the bike out and tried to pedal to work. I had ridden as far as Leece Street when bad luck struck, and I got a puncture. I couldn't get any further so I struggled home, it must have taken an hour, I sat in a chair and fell asleep. I woke up to find the kettle had boiled for so long, that it had melted, as I had left the gas on. I knew I had to get into work that day.

I struggled to finally make it to the Canada Dock. It must have been about 8am by now, and the boss gave me a right bollicking. He threatened to suspend me for three days, for not being at the Canada dry dock on time, but I persuaded him to let me off with a caution.

#4 Hatch

Thinking of the Canning dry dock brings many memories for me. We had to give the dock gateman a hand to open the dry dock gates. At that time you opened the gates by using capstans and capstan bars. But I don't think today the same method is used. At the head of the dock, where the old Liverpool Life Museum is situated today, there was an open lean-to shed where the gateman kept his gear.

In the wintertime we made a fire in a 40-gallon drum at the shed. We needed warmth to keep going after being down in the bottom of the graving dock from early morning, regulating the centre line of blocks. I experienced some good times, and some bad times.

The Tall Ships visit. This picture was taken at the Bramley-Moor and the Nelson docks

CHAPTER EIGHTEEN

Humour on the docks

The nicknames the Dockers handed out to each other were very funny.

There was **'Lino'**, "who always claimed he was on the floor" (meaning he had no money).

The **'Great Lover'** also known as **'Fill the Cot'**, "who had 10 kids".

'Perry Mason' "was always breaking into cases" (cargo).

'The Lenient Judge' "was a hatch boss, who was always shouting to let that guy go" (meaning from the ship's rigging).

'The Sick Pigeon' "was always chosen to work in the warehouse".

'The Bishop', also known as **'Bend the Bar'**, "never pulled his weight, he had his workmates on their knees. He was a lazy bloke". '

The **'Mangy Cat'** would always come out with, "I have got no fare (fur) to get home!"

'The Sly Pig' "was a man whose surname was Cunningham"

High Noon "I'm shooting off at twelve".

The **Sheriff** "Where's the hold up"?

Dr Jekyll "I need a change"

The **Spaceman** "Going to Ma's for me dinner"

There were many more nicknames. I believe Jimmy Tarbuck used some of this humour on his television shows. **'The Archbishop'** was a hatch boss. He would lean over the hatch and shout down, "A men", put them cases in the wing of the hatch!" **'Cocoa Pops'** was my father-in-law, and got his name from his sticky-out ears, which reminded you of the cereal.

There was a docker who got his son a job, he warned his son, regarding nick-names on the docks. He told him don't say a word to anybody. A week later his dad heard one of the dockers shouting to his mates to ask the **"Dummy"** (he fell for it.)

It must be said that sometimes the dockers had a really bad time of it with certain types of cargo they handled. There were wet hides that stank and very heavy bags of sugar and cases. Other cargoes were carbon black, the dreaded asbestos and other substances with more odious smells. There were no proper facilities to wash in those days. Today, there are practically no more smells, as bulk cargoes are mostly containerized, but in those days the dockers brought their smells home with them.

The Birkenhead docks was an exporting port, and had some most unusual cargoes to handle. They had some of the finest cargo boats sailing the seas at that time. There was Blue Funnel, the Clan Line, Anchor Donaldson and the Brocklebank Line which is the company which employed me.

A lot of our work was chocking off the large locomotives being shipped to the east. The south end of the docks in Liverpool were home to Elder Demsters, T&J Harrison, Palm Line, John Holt Line, Booker Line, Elders & Fifes boats sailing to West Africa, Southern United States, West Indies South America and ports throughout Europe. There were crews of many nationalities. Blue Funnel were crewed by Chinese; Clan, Anchor Donaldson and Brocklebank had Indians and T&J Harrison crewed some ships with West Indians and others with British crews. Elder Demsters, Holt, and Palm Line had West African crews, while Elders & Fifes were again British. I think that Liverpool was the largest melting pot for different nationalities in Britain. This was the making of the city.

On Friday nights, some of the apprentices went to the 'Grafton Dance'. We'd get into the dance and get our pass-out tickets, then throw our coats in the cloakroom and go over the road to the Swan Inn. The older lads had more money than us, so they paid for the ale at 10p a pint. My mate Lenny Williams was a character, and he was also a good dancer. He was always so full of life.

I remember a time when I broke my ankle playing football. I was off work for some length of time. While I was recuperating, I went to the Isle of Man to stay with my mother. During my time there, I heard that Lenny Williams had gotten into a spot of bother at work. He'd got the sack, but being Lenny, he joined the Royal Navy as a killick, and so he finished his trade as a shipwright. He was successful and given the rank of Petty Officer Shipwright, but then he had a terrible accident at Malta. He told me that as his ship was coming into harbour at the anchorage ground, in Valletta the Anchor Officer gave the order to, "Slip anchor". However, this was the wrong order, the first order should have been "Break on". The anchor cable shot along the deck, as in naval ships, the anchor cable is laid out on the fore deck. The cable dragged Lenny along the deck and tore off his right leg. That was the end of Lenny's career in the Navy.

It wasn't until some years later that I saw Lenny again. I met him in Glasgow, as he had married a Scottish lassie. He showed me his wound. However, being Lenny, he didn't let it get him down. He had an artificial leg, and moved so well, you would never have known he only had one leg. I have not seen him for more than fifty years now. I hope he is still having a good life.

La Ramona Dominica Republic Boatswain and two deck hands, M.V Walsingham

CHAPTER NINETEEN

The Army Years

I was working on the *Empress of Scotland* at the Gladstone Dock, when I heard that the ship wanted an assistant carpenter. I went up to see the Chief Officer, he informed me that had I come half an hour earlier before, I would have got the job. I was living with my Grandma Gibbons at the time and when I got home that night I found my army call-up papers had been delivered. If I had got the job on the *Empress of Scotland*, I would have been exempt from the army call up. Conscription in those days ended when you reached 26 years of age, but if you found employment at sea, you would not be conscripted into the armed forces.

I decided to join the Royal Navy on regular terms.

It meant enlisting for seven years with the flag, and five years on reserve. But after going through the motions of taking tests at St Johns Lane Naval office establishment for about six weeks, I got cold feet and decided to do my two years in the army instead. My army call up had been put back, but no sooner had I refused to join the navy, I got my army call up papers.

I arrived in Honiton after a ten hour train journey. The train went from Birkenhead Woodside station, via Exeter onto my destination to the R.E.M.E. camp in Honiton, Devon. The journey took ten hours because the train stopped at every town en route. Most of the guys were 18 year olds. This gave me the edge, being over twenty-one, and I was one of the older squaddies. I made up my mind that I was going to enjoy the two years. There was a six week basic training course. Then it was off to your respective trade training course. After you finished your course you were sent to your established camp.

After two weeks confined to camp, this was a normal routine for new intakes, we were finally allowed out of the camp. We had to be inspected by the sergeant of the guard. On returning to the camp you had to give your last three numbers to the guard commander. I had forgotten my last three numbers, for which I got a right bollocking. I was then ordered to run round the barrack square three times holding a rifle above my head. When I came back to the guard house, I still couldn't remember my last three numbers, so the sergeant screamed them in my ear. I have never forgotten those numbers! After 58 years, I still remember them: 564.

Unfortunately I had an accident on the assault course and a steel pole went into my leg. It happened in the last week of my basic training, so my posting got knocked back, I was given a cushy job in the sergeant's mess, as I had finished my basic training. One day I noticed the camp barber sniffing around the mess, the Regimental Sergeant Major nearly caught him. The barber was looking to steal some food, as rationing was still on.

Some time later, I went to the barber to get my haircut, "Just a bit off the side, barber," I requested.

He snarled at me and said, "You will get the same cut as every one else!"

Sarcastically, I said, "Will I now?" Then I told him I worked in the sergeant's mess and I had spotted him after some grub. Now I had him worried.

His attitude changed, his reply to me was, "Just a bit off the side, sir, and there will be no charge."

When I said earlier that while in the army, I was going to have more good times than bad ones, I meant it!

At this time, the Korean War was still on. While I was waiting to be posted from Honiton, my mate and I had a chance to make some cash. We were armed with two electric irons, a tin of black boot polish and a soup spoon. We went around the camp and found the new intakes and we asked them if they wanted their uniforms pressed, or to have pleats in their jackets, or to have their boots bulled-up. The second iron was for the boots, and the spoon was for rubbing the small bubbles off the leather. We got five bob to iron their jackets, and seven and sixpence to do the boots. We did plenty of trade. The electric iron that was used to bull-up the boots would be red hot; it's a wonder the stitching in the boots never fell apart.

There was a time when cleaning my rifle I got a piece of rag jammed in the breach. I was sent up to see the armourer, he asked me what trade had I been allocated to. When I told him that I had been allocated on to the armourer's course, he had a fit, and said you will never get through the armourers course while there is a hole in your arse. He looked at me and said, "I have a nice job for you!" In the armourer's workshop there was a big, cast-iron stove that was red with rust. My job was to clean it up and black lead it; that was my weekend sorted.

In my trade course, which was in Gosport near Portsmouth, I was training to be an armourer, which was one of the top trades. The armourer's job in ancient times was to build cannons, and make swords, bows and arrows. It was certainly the oldest trade in the army, it was a stiff course. There was a provost sergeant based at the camp, and he was a right bastard.

When you went out of the camp in the evening, you had to report to the guard room, which was opposite the barracks on the main road, for inspection before you went out. If this little bastard sergeant was there, look out, he would find fault with everything. You had to stand to attention while he inspected you, and you had to be presentable to the public. One Saturday, some of us were going to the football match, to see Liverpool play Portsmouth at Fratton Park. As I was running to catch the ferry for Portsmouth, I heard someone shouting "Hang on, Scouse!"

I looked back it was this provost sergeant, he was also going to the match. I remembered he was in the Seaforth Highland Regiment, so when I heard him speak, I asked, "Where's your Scottish accent gone?"

To my surprise he replied, "The only Scot in me la, is I come from Scotland Road!"

We had a good laugh at his expense and I got on alright with him after that.

I remember in the camp I had a mate called Pat Kay from the Sylvester Street area. He had been in this camp a couple of weeks before I arrived. He attempted to show me the ropes, of how easy it was to get in and out of the camp, without reporting to the guard room.

Sometimes we would avoid booking out of the camp by jumping over the railings onto the road outside the camp. That was great, until one night when we were coming back into the camp. Pat jumped over the fence without looking to see if there were any police pickets around. Unfortunately there were, and they grabbed him. I was an old arse and waited till it was clear. Later, I went in to Pat's room and he was very worried about being caught. I pulled his leg, saying, "You will get about three months." Anyway, Pat went on orders to get punished, and he ended up being discharged from the army with flat feet, so he had the last laugh on me. He was a great guy.

And yes, I passed my armourers course, with flying colours. There were twelve recruits on the course, but only four passed, I was one of the recruits who passed. I was now an armourer.

The camp at Gosport had buildings of a very strange design, I heard that it was designed to be built in India. It was two floors high with very wide and long verandas, with a flat roof. It was built in the 19th century.

I remember a time when I was taking out one of the local girls, and as were walking along a road, she had to go into the ladies' toilet. She came out with a Petty Officer's coat, which had quite a few pounds in a wallet and also had his identification book. It belonged to someone in the Royal New Zealand Navy. The girl suggested we take the money and throw the jacket away, but I didn't agree with the idea. We then took it to a police station.

We had to wait for about four hours, while the police contacted the naval yard at Portsmouth. The guy turned up looking very sheepish. He was given the coat and the lousy bugger gave me a ten bob note. I felt like telling him to stick it.

At that time I was living at my grandmother's house, but I registered my address as Tynwall Street, Douglas, Isle of Man, my mother's address; I was stationed in Weedon, Northampton. The camp was situated very handy for getting lifts home on a 48-hour pass. There were no motorways in those days, but we were at the junction of the A5 and the A45. When coming back off leave I would get the train to Coventry, then proceed to the main road outside the station, where I would thumb a lift. Incidentally, the A5 road was called, in Roman times, Whatling Street, which ran from London to Holyhead during the Roman period.

Weedon was a lousy posting. The camp was a throwback from the First World War, with tired, old, rat-infested huts. The floors were concrete, there were no mats; it was a right shit-hole of a place. The area of the camp was quite spread out as a Royal Ordinance depot. Our job in the depot was to inspect thousands of Mark 1 rifles, guns literally made for the First World War.

Working on these guns was a very boring job, so I decided to do something about it. The other R.E.M.E. lads just complained, but as usual I had to get things moving. I went to see the officer in charge, a Captain Jewel, as I recall. We had a chat, and he agreed with me on some changes. The civilian armourers didn't like it, but we had a change round. The civilians now had to inspect the old, rusty Mark 1 rifles, while we had a cushy job inspecting hand guns, which was a sitting down job. Who said there is no shop stewards in the army?

There was one time when I was waiting for a lift, a big wagon seemed to slow down for me, but he must have changed his mind and he sped off. Lousy bastard... But, five minutes later another lift stopped for me. I got aboard and the driver set off, but about five miles down the road there was a hold up, we eventually crawled past this terrible accident. It was the same lorry who had left me standing on the road. The seat I would have been sitting in was mangled up, so I do believe in fate.

Some of the things I look back on make me smile, such as one night four of us went to the local in the village. We were three Scousers and a Scotch guy named Davis. The other two Scousers were Roberts and Travis and we were coming back to the camp quite late. Just before we went into the camp, we were having a slash into the hedge, as you do. Suddenly this man appeared from nowhere, dressed in a white Mackintosh, and demanded to know what we were doing. When Jock Davis told him to fuck off, he became very insulted by the way we spoke to him and said, "Don't you know who I am?"

Jock was getting angry with this guy, I thought he was going to lamp him, but suddenly the penny dropped, and I also realized that, he was Captain Scott. Jock also realized who he was, but carried on with the bluff he said to this officer, "Let's go on up to the guard room," where there was more light. Roberts and I stayed outside the guard room, while this officer took out his credentials to show Jock and Travis. On seeing them, they sprang to attention, but they were both charged by this officer. Next morning they were on orders in front of the Commanding Officer, but he dealt with it quite leniently.

Jock Davis had four campaign ribbons on his uniform, as he had been in the navy during the war and re-enlisted in the army. I suppose this got him off with a lighter charge. At one time he had wanted to deck this arsehole, but I told him no way Jock, you'll get five years in Shepton Mallet, a severe army prison, for belting an officer.

As parading on a Saturday morning was not for me, I always volunteered to do the coal duties. All this entailed was to get a barrow of coal for our hut, which was a week's supply, It was a skive, to get out of parading.

I think that the Scousers in the army were picked on. I remember a time just before Whit leave. This Major was after someone to man the guard room, as we had three prisoners waiting to go to an army prison. So he grabbed me, for a trivial offence. I was quite good at athletics and as we were training for the sports day, I had just run the 400 metres and won. A short time later, there was the 800 metres race, and because I was last up to line up for the race, the Major put me up on a charge and said, "I told you that I was on the look out for some one to do guard duties."

I was the patsy, the fall guy. I lost my leave and I was put in charge of the prisoners. It was my duty to exercise the prisoners, which meant I had to march them around the perimeter of the camp. I would march them through the village, till we got to the village pub, the 'Wheat Sheaf'. I would say the exercise was over, we would have a few pints, and then I'd march them back up to the camp. If we had been spotted, I would have had to join them.

On Friday nights we always went up to Northampton town, where we went to a dance, but the fun started when we returned back to camp. Earlier on we made arrangements with our taxi driver to meet us at a certain spot, and then all eight of us would pile in the taxi. But instead of stopping outside the camp we made him drive into the officer's entrance. When the taxi stopped, someone would lean over and blow the horn, and then it was every man for himself and we would scarper back to our huts.

After eighteen months at Weedon I volunteered to be posted to Korea, which was duly accepted.

I was sent to Arbourfield, a transit camp where I was interviewed by the embarkation officer. He told me I had bloody cheek, because by the time I had got to Korea, it would be time for me to come back home, to be demobbed, as I had only twelve weeks to complete my national service, I knew this but it got me away from the shit hole in Weedon. But while I was at Arbourfield camp, I had a good thing going, as there was a Scouse girl working in the N.A.A.F.I. there.

I was a right spiv in those days. The ruse I had going, in the N.A.A.F.I., I would give her 3d for a cup of tea and I would get 19/9d change. After the N.A.A.F.I. closed at 9:30, we would meet in the local pub and we shared the takings. I also played a lot of football in the army, we played against the R.A.M.C., but unfortunately they had five professionals in their team and they trounced us 8-0. The rules were that they could field five professionals.

Eventually I got a very good posting, I was sent to Germany, to a little town called Lippstadt, but I was only there for eight weeks. In the village we went to the local bar, we had a great time and it didn't close. I remember that besides the beer, they made a lovely meal called "ein cutlet mit kartofl". Shortly after, my mate another armourer and I were sent to a R.E.M.E. battalion shoot, up to a place called Senalager. We spent most of our time in Senalager, which was a massive rifle range. We had our own room we didn't have to meet the sergeant till 10am to go up to the range. After Lippstadt, it was back to Aldershot in the U.K. for demobilization.

After I was demobilized, I returned to my mother's house in Douglas for a short period. I found work on the pleasure rowing boats, which lasted only one week. I would take the boats from the harbour around to the front promenade side, to the beach. Then I would tout for business, and ask the holiday people if they'd like to go rowing, or fishing on the large motor launch, or maybe for a trip to Port Soderick. But when I got my wages, I think I only got £10 after I'd been working on the beach for 10 hours a day. I said stick your rowboats as far as you can.

I suppose I was getting itchy feet; I told my mother there

was nothing for me here. I went back to my grandmother's in Liverpool, back on ship repair, but the bottom had fallen out of ship repair work.

I went to sea as an assistant ship's carpenter, as the only work going otherwise was dry-docking.

My first ship was the M.V. *Matina*, one of Elders and Fifes' banana boats. The early part of the 1950s marked the decline of ship repair on Merseyside. I would have a go at being a ships-carpenter. As work was drying up, I fancied the sea.

The squad at Honiton, R.E.M.E camp 1951
I am 2nd on the left front row

Sorry about the faded picture.
Taken at Honiton 1951,
these are members of Hut 29
at basic training camp,
I am on second row left.

Stick em up, in the armourers shop, at Lippstadt, Germany. Only four weeks till my demob, 1952

Lippstadt 1952

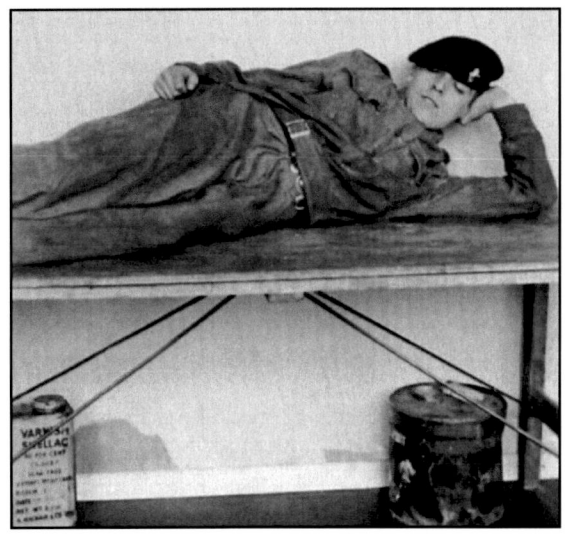

Catching up with some sleep, Lippstadt 1952

Everybody's ready for war, except me!
Germany 1952

Senalager camp with fellow armourers

Posing with my mate Steve on the rifle range 1952

CHAPTER TWENTY

A Near Disaster and Further Travel

After my time sailing on the East coast of Africa I signed on the *Athol Duke* in Bromborough Dock.

We were bound for Bahrain, for a cargo of crude oil.

The ship had a problem with the white metal bearings in the engine room. The company had sent out an engineer from UK to Bahrain to inspect the ship's engines. We had a trial run up to a port in southern Iraq, called Fao. On the way back to Bahrain, heading to the anchoring grounds, heavy laden with crude oil. There came an almighty scream from the bridge to let go the anchor. I was at my station, I threw the brake off the windlass, and the anchor and cable sped out. However, we had not reached the anchorage grounds. Therefore the water was too deep. The rubbish that shot up from the chain locker made quite a mess; the whole cable was out of the locker.

Wet Feet on The Athol Duke

The other worry was what would happen when the sea bed began to rise, when anchor took hold. The length of cable I had out was about 700 feet, how it held, I'll never know. With the weight of 20,000 tons of ship on it, the cable should have been torn apart.

The problem was they couldn't get the engine to go astern, to take the weight off the ship, so the cable stretched quite a distance astern of the ship. The ship was plagued with trouble throughout the trip.

After we left the Persian Gulf we were heading for Japan, to a city called Shimotsu, to deliver the cargo of crude oil. I will never forget that Sunday morning when most of the crew was ashore, living it up at the "Bar Rose" (a knocking shop). The ship was at its moorings, as there was no jetty to tie up to. The jetty had a floating pipe line leading from the tiny jetty to our ship. Around 9am, a very strong wind suddenly blew up. I had my port anchor out, and four lines tied to four buoys, two forward and two aft. By 11am the weather had suddenly deteriorated to storm force 10. An hour earlier, I had requested the chief officer to heave the bow end into the wind, as all the wind was on our starboard beam, but the mate wouldn't listen.

Just after 11am, all hell broke loose. The starboard rope parted, and the ship started to swing to port, dragging the port anchor out of the chain locker. I was hanging on to the brake bar, but to no avail. The captain was ashore at the agents' office, The captain and the crew could not get aboard, so the chief officer was in command. He gave orders to let the starboard anchor go, but neither of the anchors was holding. The bow of the ship went over the stern buoys, and the 12 inch oil and water pipe lines parted. The jetty was badly damaged.

The ship was like a bull in a china shop. We hit two Japanese coasters; one of them had its bridge smashed. Then the skipper was semaphoring from the shore-side to the ship to get out of the harbour, as we could do no damage while away from land, the best place is at sea. We managed to get the starboard anchor housed, but the port anchor cable twisted and the anchor jammed in the anchor recess. We sailed away from land for three days, till the storm abated, then we went back into Shimotsu to pick up the captain and crew.

*Jammed Anchor
Shimotsu Japan 1953*

We were lucky the ship never blew up. When a tanker is carrying oil and the tanks are nearly empty, it becomes much more dangerous. The fumes in the tanks only needed a spark, and the ship and all round it would have exploded. While we were at sea for the three days, the crew was based in the Bar Rose. The drinks, the women and the food were on the Captain!

We moved on to Kobe, a large port, for engine repairs. The ship still had its port anchor jammed, so I suggested we fasten a wire to the starboard anchor which was free, and let the free anchor drop to tug the port anchor free. We tried this to no avail, and the Chief Officer was resigned to give up. Then I heaved the starboard anchor further up towards the anchor recess and let go. It worked, it pulled the anchor free. The repair to the ship's engines was completed in Kobe.

While we were in Kobe, one of the crew got married by proxy. We all went to the mission church, and he took his marriage vows at 7pm. His bride back in Liverpool was at her church at 9am. We bought them a pair of Damascene vases as a gift. There was no drink in the mission, so we all went up to the Motor-Mache. This is in the city centre, for a drink. The man Tommy Schofield, who was a donkey greaser, and had been married only an hour before, was fancying a Japanese girl. We spoiled his night; we made him to go back to the ship.

We set sail for San Francisco, Wilmington and San Jose. It was a great sight to sail under the Golden Gate Bridge, as it's a very high bridge. There was a notice on one of buoys in the bay saying to all ships, *"Keep 200 yards off this point"*, as we were quite near the infamous prison Alcatraz. There is a well-known myth about the prison. The longest time spent by any prisoner on the island, was by the man known as the 'Birdman of Alcatraz', Carl Chessman. He spent 11 years there, and then he and everybody else were transferred to San Quentin.

Alcatraz went through many changes. Originally, it belonged to the Indians, and then it was a military prison. In 1933 it became a civil prison but in 1963 Robert Kennedy, who was the Attorney General at the time, closed it down. This meant that as a civil prison, it only lasted 30 years. There was never any executions took place at Alcatraz.

San Fransisco harbour is huge and deep inside the harbour there are dozens of war time built Liberty ships literally berthed at anchor alongside each other, not unlike a car lot. They were up for sale.

Now you can visit the prison by ferry as a tourist. I was surprised it was not as big as I thought. Tourists visit the island in thousands, as you can easily take the ferry from pier 39. While we were in San Francisco, I went ashore and landed up in a bar. In the bar there was a shuffle board, it looked like a large shove-halfpenny board. The bosun and I played against two other guys. One was a Chiriquí Indian, who said his name was Joe Brown, and the other guy was a jeweller. The jeweller was a pain in the arse. He kept on patronizing us, saying, "I don't know how you Brits handled all the bombing." Then he said, "We would have thrown our hands up." He told me that back in

1942, a Japanese submarine fired a couple of rounds outside the bay and broke a couple of rocks. 200,000 people evacuated San Francisco because of this, they just shit themselves, his words not mine.

At the earlier part of the trip, the captain had asked me if I was a Catholic, and then asked me how you would address a Cardinal. I told him it would be, "Your Eminence." I thought it a strange question to ask, but the reason was to be revealed later on in the trip.

As I mentioned, the ship carried at different times, both oil and molasses. To change over cargoes, you discharged your cargo of crude oil, all the tanks had to be cleaned and any trace of oil removed from the tanks. This was done between ports, after we left Japan and had discharged the crude oil. We steamed at a very slow rate of knots. Our destination was Ilo Ilo in the Phillipines. This allowed the crew time to clean the tanks before we reached our next port.

 After the tanks were completely dried out, this was done by hanging tubular wind-sails made of canvas, which were about 20 feet high and open at both ends. This would allow the air to be drawn up from the tanks. The chief officer and bosun would then go into the tank armed with hoses with hot water, to be sprayed over the insides of the tank. They both had to wear breathing apparatus with air pipes attached, and the two apprentices would pump the air to them to allow them to breathe.

I took charge of the crew, who then had to go down into the tanks. After the tanks had been hosed down, the crew used bails of old clothing, using white spirits, rubber buckets and wooden spades to clean them. This was to avoid any sparks, which given the possibility of fumes still being in the tanks could cause an explosion. We had a rig up over the tank entrance, to haul up the buckets of loose shale from the tank.

For this task the company paid us a tank cleaning bonus. It

was £20 for the crew, £25 for the boatswain and I, and £50 for the Chief Officer. It was bloody hard work. This done, we were on the way to the Philippines, to a port called Ilo Ilo, to take on molasses. The surest way to know that the tanks were cleaned, was when you could only see rust, with no dark patches.

The Philippines are made up of a thousand islands. While we were heading for Ilo Ilo, the skipper called me on the bridge. He asked me if I had taken the wheel of a ship, and saying no, he let me take the wheel. It was an awesome feeling. The ship was supposed to meet a pilot at a designated spot, but the pilot was not there, we overshot by 10 miles. We turned the ship around, The pilot was waiting for us. We arrived at this small port, on the following morning. We started loading up with molasses, and were fully loaded in 3 days. We left the Philippines after 72 hours, bound for a port named Balikpapan on the island of Borneo, for bunkers and fresh water.

I will never forget Borneo! The skipper asked me to try a bottle of their local drink so I took a swig; it was the worst firewater I had ever drunk. The crew was also supping this stuff called "King Rum". It blew your bloody head off. The crew was so drunk, it took them three days to sober up. We left port having to manage without the crew, as they were not compos mentis (pissed as newts). The crew was so drunk, one of them collapsed in the alleyway and there were footprints on him. They really were drunk for three days, and some of the engineers and stewards had to help on deck to let go of the ropes of the ship leaving the port.

We were bound for Sydney with a cargo of molasses, when we reached a small island called Thursday Island, south of New Guinea, where we picked up two pilots to take the ship down the Great Barrier Reef. You could see the sharks swimming quite near to the ship. At places you can see the Barrier Reef not 100 yards away. If we went too close, the sharp reef would do some damage to the ship. It was a three-day trip down to

Sydney. Sydney's harbour is very large, but they had not yet built the world famous Opera House. I noticed that the famous Sydney Harbour Bridge was built by Dorman Long of Glasgow.

We set sail for San Francisco across the Pacific Ocean, half way across you lost a day, crossing the International Date Line, as east meets west of the hemisphere.

On that trip we had a crew member called Jimmy Smiler. He was smiler by name, smiler by nature. He was quite a character, always ready for a laugh. While we were at San Francisco, everybody had to be vetted by the doctor and the C.I.A. before anybody could go ashore. But Jimmy had been deported back in 1938, and according to their records, Jimmy was not allowed to go ashore in the States. I think he had jumped ship in New York one time before. They had a C.I.A. security guard at the foot of the gangway to prevent Jimmy from getting off the ship. The bay in San Francisco is huge. There was an area in the bay that had about 30 liberty freighters anchored, of which I mentioned earlier in the book like a car lot, waiting for someone to buy them. The price was I believe was $100,000 each.

Jimmy certainly made up for San Francisco, when we got to Sydney. The ship was berthed alongside a smaller vessel, at a very wide old wooden quay. Jimmy had gone ashore for the first time in eight weeks, and we watched him coming back to the ship, after he had had his booze, he was legless. Being a very tall and a very thin man, he seemed to be bent over at the hips, but he never once fell over. He zigzagged from one side of the quay to the other, and we were taking bets that he would go in the 'oggen' (sea), but he managed to get up the two gangways.

He crossed the deck of our ship, and still he never fell over, till he got to his cabin, and then bugger me, he tripped over the step to his quarters, splitting his head open on the iron bunk bed. He sustained a bad wound over his eye, but refused to go to the hospital to get stitched up. He was a hard man, and was back on the job next day. He always sang "Stay in your own back yard", an old southern Negro song, and he had quite a repertoire.

Then there was the time when the desalination tank had a problem. The desalination tank is used for the cooling of the ship's engine. Salt sea water is taken in and after the salt has been removed, the water is circulated around the ship's engine. There were two 12-inch pipes, one going in and one coming out. There was a fracture in the pipe, which meant water was cascading into the engine room, and the only way to have a temporary repair was to encase it in cement. We had to stop the ship's engines before I could fix the cement box around the fracture, as there was too much vibration from the engines. I decided to use soda ash to make the cement dry quicker, it worked and after an hour it set, then we were on our way.

There is no finer sight than to see the albatrosses in flight they seem to come from nowhere, some have a wingspan of 12 feet. They can stay out at sea for weeks at a time. They never seem to flap their wings, but just glide in and out of the troughs. You know when you start getting nearer land, as the birds simply vanish.

I remember when we going down the Red Sea, we ran into a storm of locusts, literally thousands of the buggers. They were everywhere, all over the rigging, everywhere. I laughed when the third mate grabbed a handful of locusts and put them in one of the cadet's bunks.

A tanker sits quite low in the water. All tankers have a shallow freeboard, and when there is a big sea running you're like a submarine. I asked one of the stewards to close his port light and pull his dead light down. He didn't take my advice, and all of a sudden a big solid tube of water came through his porthole. It took just seconds to have two feet of water in their cabin. Their clothes and their bedding were all soaked; it was a classic case of, "I told you so". When the weather is very bad, the deck hands have to fix up the life lines along the deck. These are taut wires running from the accommodation to the bridge section. You then have a nine inch piece of rope with a round steel becket in, which it fits around the taut wire.

We finally reached Sydney to discharge the cargo of molasses. While we were in Sydney, one of the stewards introduced his father to me. I was curious to know why he was living in Sydney, and he told me he had jumped ship twelve months ago. I thought that would be the last time I would ever see him, but read on.

Sydney 1953 the Athol Duke

We left Sydney and sailed back up the Barrier Reef, heading for Thursday Island to drop off the two pilots. It's a three-day trip up the Barrier Reef, and after we left Thursday Island, we went on to Java.

The next port of call was Surabaya to load molasses for Genoa, Italy. The weather in Java was 42 degrees centigrade. It was a sticky heat, and you couldn't stop sweating. To cool off, we asked the engineer to put the water on deck, where we stood under the fire hydrants to us to cool down.

While we were alongside in Surabaya, I was looking over the stern at the 14-foot sand sharks. I had a thin wire with a piece of meat tied to a meat hook. The wire went over the pulley fastened to the after davit. We had the wire turned round the drum of the after mooring winch and waited, but after a few hours we got fed up. Then, one of the sharks bit the bait and I shouted, "Turn on the steam!" We had half of the shark out of the water, it gave up the ghost, no fight whatsoever. I put a running bowline round the wire, dropped it over the head, worked it towards the tail and turned it upside down, using a snatch block we heaved it on deck and the local workmen asked if they could have the shark. They cut it up in pieces and the back bone was given to the skipper, it was shaped like a walking stick.

The boatswain and I went ashore for a drink. It was a long walk to get out of the refinery, and it was about half a mile to the main gates. While we were sitting outside of a bar we noticed one of our crew, Tony Monti. Tony had gone ashore on his bike, but for some unknown reason he was stopped and searched by the police. At that time the country was under Communist rule and you were not allowed to carry too much money. He was arrested. The skipper and the company agent had to go and get Tony out of gaol.

They had to bribe the head of the police with 10,000 cigarettes, and after his release, Tony was told in no uncertain manner to get your arse back to the ship. Sitting on the veranda of the pub, we spied Tony. He was coming towards us with a crowd of Javanese people, who were looking with envy at his bicycle. (When the Dutch had this colony, they introduced the bicycle to that part of the world.) Tony's bike was a fine racing bike, and as we didn't have much cash on us, we persuaded Tony to sell his bike to the highest bidder. As he got a good price for it, this was our chance to get a loan off Tony as we were broke.

We didn't get back to ship till the next morning, we were nearly (beached) stranded, as the ship had already dropped its ropes and was ready to sail. We had to board the ship by motorboat, we were lucky, as in another ten minutes we would have been ten displaced seamen. I got a right bollocking off the skipper, who said I should have had more sense, being the ship's carpenter. I was lucky I never got logged, which meant a day's pay would have been stopped. We set sail for Genoa and reached our destination, it took us three weeks, as we were still having trouble with the ship's engines. Genoa is a beautiful port, with so much architecture to be seen. I had been there before, in the *Bothnia*.

Earlier in the trip, knowing I was a Catholic, the skipper had asked me about how you would address a Cardinal, and now I found out why. The ship had a special visitor. It was Cardinal Giuseppe Roncalli, Genoa's Cardinal, with whom we all got to shake hands.

Little did we know he would shortly become Pope John 23rd, who was my favourite Pope. He was a small man and very friendly towards the crew. He was the Pope who convened Vatican 2 and turned the Catholic Church on its head, by telling the religious to go into the world and live in the real world, not to live behind walls. He told them that it takes more than just prayer alone. It was great to have met him. This ship of ours had gone through some bad times before I joined it. It is possible the ship needed some blessing.

The story has it that the trip before I joined, when the ship was heading home to the U.K, there came orders to return to the Persian Gulf to pick up a cargo of crude oil. As the ship had been away from the U.K. for a very long time, the crew was looking forward to some home leave. When they heard the new orders, the crew mutinied. The British Navy put out a ship from Gibraltar. They boarded her, took the ringleaders off, and the main culprit got three years in goal. Also during that trip, an engine greaser fell down in the engine room and was killed. They had to bury him at sea. The ship was jinxed. It needed some blessing!

We set sail for Greenock. As I said earlier, one of the stewards, called Charley, had introduced his father to me in Sydney. As I came down the gangway, I noticed a familiar looking guy standing on the quay. I told a steward, who was in the same cabin as Charley that I was sure I had seen Charley's dad. He told me, that we'd had him aboard all the way home from Sydney. I found it unbelievable that you could stow away on a tanker, this takes some nerve. Taking into account the very hot temperatures in Java, the captain's weekly inspections around the crew's quarters, and our few days in Genoa, I would say that beats any record of a stowaway, on any ship.

I had a problem getting my luggage home, as not only did I have the usual presents like Japanese dinner and tea sets, but the skipper and I had bought a load of Javanese teak between us. I had to use a small wagon to take it to the railway station in Greenock, and send it home by rail. I was really glad to get home this time; we had been away for ten months.

I next shipped out on a P.S.N.C boat called the *Walsingham*, a small passenger cargo ship sailing to Hamilton in Bermuda, then on to Havana in Cuba. This was during the time when Batista was in power. He was a corrupt gangster which suited the United States. Shortly after Castro overthrew the crooked governmental dictatorship of Batista. The United States has had an embargo on Cuba for the last 47 years.

During the Wilson government, the U.K. was sending a consignment of buses to Cuba, but the ship was sabotaged. There is a strong suspicion that it could have been the C.I.A. that scuttled the merchant ships in the River Thames.

This was during the time when the Kennedy government nearly started World War 3. The Americans called Khrushchev's bluff when the Russians were sending missiles to Castro. As the Russian ships were carrying missiles for Castro and were getting nearer to Cuba, the American Navy had orders from Washington to sink these ships if they reached Cuban waters. This deterred Khrushchev, who withdrew the ships back to Russia. Everyone heaved a huge sigh of relief. At the same time, the Americans had missiles strategically placed around Russia in countries like Greece, Turkey, West Germany, Norway and other Far East countries.

But what of Cuba today, although there is still a lot of poverty in Cuba it is said that they have some of the best health care in the world, and education is far better there today. After the missile crisis, and without the pressure of the United States, naturally Cuba would have fared much better. But I hope the Americans elect Barack Obama as the next President, and that he will lift the embargo on Cuba. The camp at Guantanamo also must go… However, tourism is very good and is a thriving industry in Cuba now. As I write this, President Obama has been elected, and hopefully regarding Cuba, restrictions will be lifted, after 48 years of living under an embargo.

Our ship was loaded with bulk sugar at San Antonio and was brought to the quayside by a small locomotive pulling trucks of bagged sugar. The train was built in Glasgow in the late 19th century. The fuel for the train was the compressed leaves of the sugar. It gave off a sweet smell.

Homeward bound, the Chief Officer of the ship was younger than I. He was a good Chief Officer, there was no side to him. He asked me come back next trip. But I had decided to swallow the anchor, I'd had enough. I wanted to come ashore, so I signed off for good.

CHAPTER TWENTY-ONE

Some Amazing Stories

I knew a man by the name of Gus Swinson, who lived near me in Dingle Mount. He claimed to be the longest Liverpool survivor in an open life boat. He was torpedoed, and found himself alone, when all the other men in the boat had died. He was 72 days adrift, but was rescued by none other than a German U-boat, every crew member of the U-boat, were amazed of his resilience, and treated Gus as one of their own, Gus was now a prisoner of war, but when the war had ended, the Captain of the U-boat always kept in touch with Gus.

A drinking partner, Peter Ryan, was in the second ship that was to be sunk during the war. It was 1939 in a ship called the *Trevelyan*, a Royal Mail boat. She was sunk by the famous German pocket battle ship, the *Admiral Graf Spee*.

The commander of the battleship was Captain Lansdorf, if it was possible he ordered the crews of the ships that were to be sunk to take to the lifeboats, as he had chosen not to take lives. Peter was taken aboard the German Battleship, and remained on board for 12 weeks. He was then transferred to the German prison ship, the *Altmark*, to take the prisoners back to Germany as P.O.W, but as the *Altmark* was proceeding up the English Chanel, to her destination, the Royal navy ship, the H.M.S *Cossack*, intercepted the *Altmark*. The Royal Marines boarded her, and released the prisoners, then sank her.

Peter returned home, and went back to sea. He died in 1998.

I remember a time when I was having a pint with Granddad Gibbons, a man came in the pub, and he introduced me to him.

After a chat, when he had gone, Granddad told me he was one of the Liverpool V.Cs, won in the 1st World War. He wouldn't talk about it. This was Billy Radcliffe, he wiped out a machine gun nest at the battle of the Mons.

A school mate of mine "Dessy" Fox, was given awards for his valour at the Korean War in 1949,

The story he related to me was that Des was a private in the famous regiment, The Glorious Gloucesters, and had lost contact with his battalion. He hid under a house for three days, ventured out, only to be caught by a small band of North Koreans, as the story goes. Des being a big lad, the soldier who was in command of the North Koreans set up a contest, and selected his biggest man to fight by unarmed combat; if Des won, he could go free. Des defeated his opponent, he said he knocked the shit out of him. The Korean kept his word, Des eventually got back to his Battalion. I met Des some years after ans quizzed him about it, as it was in the National press. He told me it was a load of bollocks, Des could spin a yarn. He returned to the Isle of Man, and was given a civic reception by the Governor, Des could carry a good tale.

CHAPTER TWENTY-TWO

Swallowing the Anchor

I came home and got a job in a boat-building firm by the name of P. Winram, which was in Caryl Street. The company was established over 100 years; the building we worked in was probably over 200 years old. It was an old warehouse during the 18th and 19th century, there were three basements, but the basements were impassable. I believe they used to serve the Brunswick Dock by connecting with underground passageways.

Winram had a contract with Cock Tugs, under which we repaired the wooden fenders, called the 'rubber', which ran around the tug. The timber that we worked with, was wet elm, and you can only work with this timber when it is wet. The wooden fender was used to push the ships in and out of the docks. The fenders were constantly being damaged. This type of work was tooled by adze work, you had to fashion the timber to suite the shape of the tug.

I remember working at Winram's with a friend called Bob Williams. He told me an amazing tale. He had fought in the First World War and was assigned to the Royal Signals Regiment. He told me how he nearly got sentenced to be shot during the Battle of Mons.

He had been at his post for 36 hours with no sleep, when he happened to nod off. An officer, who for some reason didn't like Bob, found him asleep and said, "I have you now, Roberts," and charged him with being asleep on duty. He told me he was shitting himself; it was to be a Field Court Marshall. He was found guilty, normally this offence carried a death sentence.

Bob was sentenced to be tied hand and foot spread eagled to the gun carriage wheel for 90 days. He was tied spread eagled from sunrise to sunset, but he considered himself lucky, not being shot. Bob always seemed to have a nervous disposition, now I know why.

It was a funny coincidence, Eileen and I went to see the Granddaughters appearing in the school musical, it was "Oh What a Lovely War". The play is a dig at the war mongers, at the need to go to war!

I worked for Winram's for about 18 months. I remember one day when we told the apprentices to bring the tools and the gear down to the west side of the Queen's Dock. They, being lads, were arsing about and they accidentally pushed the handcart into the dock. We had to use grappling hooks to try and retrieve the tools. We managed to rescue some of tools, and the lads got a right bollocking from us.

I had a good run at Winram's, till the work went slack, then it was back to the dole. When there was no work, you had to report to the Labour Exchange (dole) every day, including Saturday morning. The office was on Regent Road, near the Canada Dock. You saw a man by the name of Mr. Hammond to sign on. This was going on the pool. There could be a hundred shipwrights reporting for work, this was very casual work, where you could be employed for as many as six or more firms in the one week. This work was dry docking and undocking ships, known as shoring and unshoring. The pay was a full day's pay for drydocking a ship, and half a day's pay for taking the ship out of the dry dock.

They could pay for regulating the bottom of the dry dock, to prepare the centre blocks that the ship sits on, these had to be level. The centre line on the bottom of the dry dock had wedge-shape castings which were about four-feet long. These were made of cast iron and were very heavy, with each casting weighing about 180 kilos. These castings could be moved up or down as they were wedge shaped, by using a large crow bar, till they were level with each other. The wooden dock blocks were then dogged (fastened) to the iron castings, three inch thick wooden capping tied on top of the blocks using spun yarn (spun yarn was covered with Stockholm tar). Even at these times you found things amusing, such as there could be as many as 20 men pulling the heavy timber shores or props out of the dry dock. You always had a caller shouting, all together lads, "Heave-ho!" Lads… some of them would be in their eighties! Imagine pulling a rope with a gang of men, with the rope being the shape of the letter Z, most of the weight was taken up by the younger men.

Some of these men served in the First World War. There were some of them who served in the Boer War. These older men returned to work during the war years, as the younger men were away in the services. They filled the gap.

The Mersey Docks and Harbour Board had a large fleet of hoppers and dredgers, and at that time they had the largest dredger in the world, named the *Leviathan*. She was built during the First World War and unlike the other dredgers who had two cranes, she had two massive suckers on either side. There were other types of dredgers, such as bucket dredgers, which had two huge steel guides with a series of buckets that rotated on a never-ending chain. A Dutch company called The Westminster Dredging Company, which worked the Mersey for many years, had a very large bucket dredger called the *Europer*.

One of the dirtiest and heaviest jobs was to dry dock these dredgers. They were either at the Canning, Herculaneum or the Clarence dry docks. The main trouble with them was that when they dropped their bottom doors, there was mud everywhere. They had to be hosed down before you could start any work on them, but there was plenty of work to be had on these vessels.

The Dock Board also had large floating cranes including the Mammoth, which was the largest floating crane in the world in its day. The Dutch built it before the First World War, but it had to be scuttled during the Second World War in the Birkenhead docks, as it would have been a landmark for German bombers. The crane had to have four tugs when she crossed the river, but she could manoeuvre herself in the docks. She was built in Holland in 1912 and taken by the Germans in the First World War. After the war ended she was taken over by the Mersey Dock Board, then during the eighties she was bought back by the Dutch.

The other two floating cranes were the *Atlas* and the *Titan*. The *Titan* crane had to be driven by the ship's steam she was working at, as they had to link up to the ship's steam pipe. If she was lifting anything heavy and the steam was lost, the crane could not lift. The *Titan* used a chain, instead of wire cable. This crane should have been in the museum.

One of the Dock Board tenders was the *Galatea*. She was very old, but she was a beautiful ship. Built like a yacht, she opened the Gladstone dry dock in 1923 when King George V attended.

On the Gladstone west side they had a fog horn called the Bootle Bull. When it went off you could hear it for miles, but it is no more. At times I saw three Cunard liners abreast of each other in Huskinsson No. 1. The dock was so loaded you could walk from ship to ship, from one side of the dock to the other side.

I worked on the *Skirmisher*, a Cunard tender which was in the Clarence dry dock. One of the scalers was chipping its paint and his chipping hammer went through the side of the ship! After inspection, the ship was for the knackers yard, but she had had a long life; at 70 years they got their money's worth. She was well built for the time; I noticed her hull plates were fashioned in one piece, no plates were butted. In other words, all the plates went from the stem to stern, and were all riveted. There was no welding in the 19th century.

The next job was at Cammell Laird's, where I worked on building submarines in the south yard. I was on permanent nights; I worked the 7pm till 7am shift. It was heavy work, but it could be interestingly intricate work. The money was also a bit better. It came in handy, as I was getting married to Eileen.

In Cammell Laird's while I was working on submarines, you got used to noise, as the submarine inner shell is completely round. The steel caughers were ve-ing the plates, to be welded it was like being in a drum, you never heard the noise after a while, you got used to the din, there was no protection for your ears or head gear.

One job I did like, was on the launch day. The keel of the sub would be sitting on three-inch wooden caps, and we used sharp steel wedges to split the caps away. You could hear the groan of the submarine lowering itself onto the slip way. When all the caps were cut free, the huge, long hardwood wedges were rammed under the wooden launch standing ways. The wooden launch ways that took the ship into the water sat on the standing ways, on either side of the ship. There was a slot in the standing ways, on which there were two huge triggers which prevented the launch ways from moving down the slip way. When the naming took place, the triggers were dropped allowing the launch ways and the ship to enter the river.

I must mention that all ships that are built on a slipway have a declivity, or fall of 5/8ths to the foot. This in essence means that there would be quite a steep slope before it hits the water. Cammell Laird's yard is one of the best yards to launch a ship, mainly because of the river's strong current. The launch takes place just after high water. There is no need for drag chains, which other shipbuilding yards have to use, to arrest the ship after she hits the water. This is because the River Mersey is quite wide, with a strong nine knot current.

When I look back at the shipbuilding industry, there was too much protectionism regarding each tradesman's job. At

Cammell Laird's we had a dispute between the Shipwrights and the Boilermakers union, of who should twang the chalk line. Although I was a trade unionist, we cut our own throat by having these demarcation issues. The Japanese and Koreans didn't have any demarcation problems.

The British shipbuilding yards lost many contracts to yards abroad by using old fashioned methods.

The foreign yards were using modern ideas, and moved ahead of British shipbuilding.

Shipbuilding in Britain has never recovered.

The good news is as I write, Cammell Laird's is being brought back from extinction, and has concrete orders for many millions of pounds of work from the Government to refurbish naval ships. The yard had been ticking over by a company called the North Western Shipbuilding Company, but the name Cammell Laird is a world renowned name. They now need apprentices to be trained up to help in making Birkenhead the shipbuilding centre for the North West again.

I never liked working in Cammell Lairds. I had to catch the underground at James Street station to Green Lane, dash down Green Lane then try to get across the New Chester Road, which was very busy with traffic. The time-keepers would see us from across the road, so the lousy buggers would slam the gates shut. You then had to wait till they opened them again at 8.15am and you would be booked in late. If you lost time twice in the month, you had to go home and this meant you lost half a day's pay. In the winter working on the slipways was very hard as a cold wind came in off the River Mersey. We used 40 gallon drums in which to make a fire. Sometimes Charlie Chase (as we called the yard manager) would kick the fire drums over. He was an old bastard; nobody liked him. Your hands would stick to steel as it was bitterly cold to handle. Hot water for making tea was provided at lunch time. The taps would be turned on at the stroke of noon, and never before noon, they had it off to a fine art.

CHAPTER TWENTY-THREE

Our European Tour

I met up with two of my old mates from the army, and the three of us decided to go touring the continent in Barney's car, it was a A55 Austin.

I remember a priest, a Father Vicario from Mount Carmel church, whom I knew and became very friendly with, and he had heard of our plan to go touring. The priest and I went to meet two of my friends one night at the George Hotel in Lime Street. The market car park is there today.

He asked if he could come along. He would be an asset, as he could speak French. This was OK by us, but a few weeks before we were ready to go, the priest had to call it off. We three, Barney, Mally and I, set off to France in Barney's Austin A55. We went through France to Switzerland, then on to Italy, heading for Genoa. The drive on the Italian motorway was quite scary. It was at night and the problem we had was that all the heavy goods wagons were going the opposite way with their headlights on full beam. This meant we had to drive dazzled all the way to Genoa.

We arrived in Genoa very late and bleary-eyed. We stayed two days. I had been there before, while at sea some years ago. I took my mates to the seedy parts to see the bars with the prostitutes hanging around. I think that I frightened them. Then it was off to Monte Carlo. We took in the sights of how the rich lived. Two days later we headed off to Macon and arrived in the early evening. We decided to have a drink and then get back to the hotel. We had a long journey ahead of us to Paris the next day. While we were in this bar, an elderly French guy was eying us up. He asked if he could join us. That was alright by us. Later on, as he could speak no English, he kept on saying to us, "Comstar, comstar!" I twigged that he meant come with him to another bar. He was a little bit over the top with the booze. When we came out the bar we saw he had a big, new, top-of-the-range Citroen. As soon as he got in the driver's seat, he appeared to sober up.

A barmaid in the next bar told us that he was the richest man in the province. We therefore kindly let him pay for the drinks. We ended up in a tiny bar, just the three of us and the landlady. It was 2.30am. We got back to our hotel about 3.00am, so much for our early night! It was midday before we set off for Paris.

We finally arrived in Paris in the late evening, where we found accommodation at a hotel situated in Rue Cambon. Rue Cambon was at the back of The Ritz hotel. Many years later in the nineties, Princes Diana was televised coming out of the rear entrance of The Ritz, which was owned by Al Fayed. This was the last time she was seen alive, before being driven to her death.

Incidentally, to get back to Father Vicario, I had a incident with him, as I lived at my grandma's and slept in the bedroom which had its window on the landing.

While in bed I heard a tapping on the window, it would be about 5-30am. I got up and opened the door, only to find this priest. I asked "What the hell are you doing at this time of the morning?" He seemed a bit shifty, I realised he had been up to no good and I asked him "Have you been with a woman?", and he was half boozed. I then told him, "Why don't you take off your collar, as it looks like you have lost the priesthood". He said "I don't give a fuck". I thought it was a very sad affair.

The same priest later succumbed to the wiles of a prostitute in Picadilly, Manchester and was fined £10. This was reported in the local press. He left the church in disgrace. I thought it sad, and I cannot understand this ancient rule of celibacy, which was introduced way back in the 13th century when the religious were allowed to marry. The Catholic Church is very slow to change, but I believe it will.

I know a number of priests who have left the priesthood, and have married, have a family, and are quite happy.

The idea of celibacy was that the priest would be married to the church, but the way that the church moves it will be another 50 years before its changed back as it was.

CHAPTER TWENTY-FOUR

My Grandma

I lived with my grandma for about eight years. She lived on the top landing of the flats, while I worked on the docks. I remember she had a big round table with an oil cloth table cover, and sitting around the table with my Granddad, Joey, Jimmy and Tommy and the topic of discussion was the docks. They were all dockers, with the exception of Tommy, who worked in the office at the Shell Mex Dingle oil jetty, and I, a shipwright. The banter would be about loading and unloading ships. Tommy got a cob-on (his knickers in a twist) and he would say, "For Christ's sakes, beam up, and put the hatch-boards on! We're having our tea here." Meanwhile, my poor old Grandma had to sit in the background waiting at their beck and call. I always felt sorry for her; the household was totally male oriented. I always took her side.

Thursday night was dockers' pay night. Most Thursdays no overtime was worked, so they were all home by five o'clock. One night, Grandma was nowhere to be found, she had gone into town to get some shopping, as she did regularly. However, my Nin liked a Guinness or two. It got to 7.30 when there was a knock on the door. A large lady was standing there, asking, "Does this lady live here?" and Grandma came trotting in. Although she was only 4 feet 10 inches, she could stand up for herself. She always wore a black shawl, and whatever meat she had bought had cooked under her arm. Then the shit hit the fan, my grandfather would bellow, "Where the hell have you been, you drunken cow?"

In those days a woman's job was washing, ironing and cooking, and having kids.

Grandma never had a holiday in her life. My mother told me that Granddad use to give her many hidings. If Everton got beaten, there would be trouble, but this type of thing happened in many households in those days. This night in question, the air was blue, and he was saying things like, "Where is my tea? Where have you been? You drunken cow!" I took her side, and told him to leave her alone, but she always fought for the last word. Her excuse was she had had a blackout in Lime Street and she was taken up to the hospital, where the doctor gave her some brandy to revive her. But I ask you, why couldn't the men ever cook their own meals? However, that's the way things were.

My Grandma had a colostomy in 1939, and for 20 years she wore a wide colostomy belt. When a district nurse visited my Grandma, the nurse threw a fit about this contraption that had been given to my Grandma, as this idea was done away with many years before. She should have had a colostomy bag fitted years ago, but she was now in her seventies. The nurse played merry hell with her doctor. Shortly afterwards they tried to fit her with one at home. I was in the kitchen when I heard an unearthly scream from Grandma. It didn't work and the poor soul had to carry on by emptying her bowels leaning over the bath, and then clean up after herself. There were many times I had to stand on the landing outside the front door, because the smell was so bad, but it was not her fault.

It was my grandfather's idea to live in these tenements, and to live on the top landing, as he stupidly thought the air was fresher living on the top landing. When he grew older this would be a great burden climbing eight flights of stairs. Grandma used to have rows with him, and she blamed him for taking this house. She wanted to live in a decent house, as they could afford it because they were all working.

My grandfather died in 1958. After he died, my grandma went into her shell and never spoke a word, even after the way he had treated her down through the years. She followed him 12 months later. It was sad the way she deteriorated, she had been somebody so full of fun and life. I remember an old mate of hers, Mrs Maclinden, who used to call on her. Granddad never liked her. She was the pop star Gerry Marsden's grandmother, and there were times when a very young Gerry called to our house asking for his grandma, and granddad would chase him away. My grandma and his grandma really liked a Guinness or two, and a pinch of snuff. Grandma also liked a gamble on the horses, but when she lost, Gordon Richards the famous jockey (his parents were never married), She called him a little bastard, as she always backed him to win.

The only time she enjoyed herself was when her son Tommy ran a football sweep. One day in the year, everyone who was part of the sweep went on an outing to Blackpool. She really had a good time. Fred and Mary Marsden played the banjo and supplied the music on the coach. I suppose this is where Gerry got his music from.

In the days when we were kids, we had to go up the back entry, and go in the back door to Grandma Stamper's, in Dombey Street. Granddad Stamper had this terrible asthma which he contracted when he was gassed at the Battle of Mons in the First World War. He didn't live beyond 60 years old, but he still smoked about 40 cigarettes a day. This helped him on his way. I remember going to Grandma Stamper's house, back in the thirties. My brother and I would often cut along High Park Street, and proceed down a tiny street called Sefton Square. St. Peter's was on the corner, and this street led to a farmyard. This had a right of way that led into Amity Street via North Hill Street and down Windsor Street to Dombey Street. Grandma lived in number 72.

It was quite a posh place to us kids, as we were only used to a tiny two up and two down gas-lit house, with plenty of mice for company. I was eight when I left Byles Street. Those houses were built in the middle of the 19th century, St. Paul's School was built in the 1840s. It had its own church, St. Paul's, in Belvedere Road, that had a lovely tall slim spire, which backed on to Prince's Park. But alas, it was pulled down some years ago due to a loss of worshippers, as is the trend in today's society. It is a known fact that Liverpool had more churches per mile, than any other city in the country.

At the corner of Byles Street and Hawkstone Street was the Railway Mission Hall, they were called the Christian Volunteers. There were plenty of charabanc day outings in the summer days.

The small shop at the corner of Byles Street and Hawkstone Street, was a lovely little sweet shop, the owner was Lesbulls, and they sold sweets quite cheaply at 1/2d for a little bag, such as Uncle Joes Mint balls, Acid drops, Dolly mixtures, and many more niceties.

CHAPTER TWENTY-FIVE

Ship's Carpenter

Now I had finished with the army, I decided to sign on to go to sea as a ship's carpenter. For my first trip I was the carpenter's mate on the *Matina*, an Elders & Fifes banana boat. We set sail for Kingston, Jamaica and loaded up with a cargo of bananas at Port Antonio.

The sight of the loading was amazing. The ship had large side doors, which opened to allow the cargo to be stowed in both sides of the ship. There was a large barge, with a 20 foot load high of bananas, which came along to the off-side of the ship, so that the ship would be loaded on both sides.

The workers carried to the loading gangway the full stalk of bananas. There was a man sitting on a trestle with a large, sharp panga (knife). As the workers passed him, he would slice the stems of the bananas off. They would then run past a counter machine, pulling a little chord with a 'ding'. ("As in the West Indian calypso, Tally me, Tally me, Tally me banana.") The ship was loaded within 48 hours. The hatches were sealed, as these ships were refrigerated.

Leaving Port Antonio was a work of art. The ship had to go astern and literally bend itself round the end of the quay, until it was at right angles to the quay, before it could slide off into the open sea. After 24 hours at sea on the return voyage, we heard knocking from the hatches. When we opened them up, we found stowaways in all the hatches. The poor buggers had only skimpy shorts and tatty vests to wear, and were freezing. All 17 were men, were fed, and given some old clothes. Some blankets and locked up in the forecastle storeroom. Unfortunately I had to take forepeak soundings, and the forepeak sounding pipe was where the stowaways were locked up. The stench was bad but what could we expect? There were no urinals.

The stowaways were put to work. As the ship had wooden decks, they were told to holystone the decks. Stones about 10x6x4in were pulled and pushed across the decks, fastened to long broom handles, sand was spread on the wooden decking also water, which made the wooden decks look grand.

Grinding coffee in the end of a tree trunk, at La Ramona A native dock canteen, M.V Walsingham 1954

They were entertaining, as they would make up melodies while working. It was good to listen to. I found that out of 17 stowaways, 6 had no official landing papers. I laughed when one of them told me that the last ship he had stowed away on, never went to the U.K. at all, but to New York. He was sent back to Jamaica and goaled for six months. However, this time he had his papers and so would be free to go in the U.K.

When we reached Southampton, the police came on board to take the stowaways away. The six with no papers were sent back to Jamaica and gaoled for six months. One of them told me how he was going to be a bouncer in a London club. I often wonder where they are now, 55 years later. The normal procedure was that after serving their time in gaol, the men would make their way to an organization run by Sir Leary Constantine, where they were given what they needed to move on and rebuild their lives.

I had taken this job as assistant carpenter's mate just to get the first stamp in my book, but now I could take a carpenter's job in my own right.

I signed on the M.V. *Wayfarer* as carpenter, a *Harrison* boat bound for East Africa. After we left Liverpool, the first port was Berbara in British Somaliland. When we arrived, it looked like a moonscape and was very hot. There was no jetty, so we had to discharge the cargo over the side of the ship, into a large Dhow. The cargo was then taken to the quayside about half a mile away. Camels on the quay took some of the cargo away into the desert, I don't know where.

Wayfarer 1954 "Home Sweet Home"

Sailing out of South Africa, the first port after Lorenzo Marques was Durban, this was the first time I saw a rickshaw. There were two types of rickshaws, one that was pulled by a Zulu in full regalia, which was for whites only, and another type where the man was attired in brown shirt and shorts, for Indians only. To be transported by rickshaw was an experience! They could really move. They would run 50 yards then leap in the air and cover about another 50 yards treading fresh air. However, it's said that the men who pulled the rickshaws had a short life span, as it affected their hearts.

In 1956 President Nasser took over in Egypt, after the coup of King Farouk, who was thrown out of Egypt. Nasser decided to take over the running of the Suez Canal, which at that time was run by the British and the French. Britain invaded the Suez Canal area; this was an arrogant mistake made by the British. These were troubled times in Egypt, the British army had to leave Egypt. The British Prime Minister at the time was Sir Anthony Eden. The American President Eisenhower demanded the British army to get the hell out of Egypt, as we had no right being there. Eden was a disaster; he was the Foreign Secretary under Winston Churchill during the war.

M.V Assyria, Cunard line, on the Montreal run

Zanzibar was the next port, then, we sailed on to Mombasa, Kenya. This was a good place to go ashore, as there was plenty of music and places to relax. The best times were had in the Star Bar. One time, we went ashore up the Kilindili road to the Star Bar and we were having a quiet drink, minding our own business. Suddenly, the fun kicked off. We watched a battle; British soldiers were fighting amongst themselves. The band played on, as chairs and tables were thrown. I think the soldiers were probably enjoying themselves! Mombasa was a thriving and up-and-coming port. McAlpines were building a new port, with fine wide quays.

While we were berthed in Mombasa, I asked the cook not to throw any food away, as the dockworkers wanted the leftovers. I put the food on a big tray; roast potatoes, meat, vegetables, prunes, custard and everything. They devoured the lot with relish. There was a castle boat docked ahead of us. She was a big passenger ship called the *Durban Castle*. During the evening, a crewmember from the Castle boat came aboard our ship carrying a case of lager. He came into the pump man's room, but then we realized he was bent as a 4-pound note, we had a good laugh. This man was the queen of the *Durban Castle*. After a short while, I went out of the room to go to the toilet. I was confronted by one of the firemen, who told me to lay off, as he had his eye on the gay guy. I was amazed; he meant it! I said, "If it pleases you, get in there!"

One evening they had a gala aboard the Castle boat with a band. All the gays were dressed in their evening gowns. I missed a good night by not going. The Castle liners had a big complement of gays; I suppose regarding homosexuality, we were too narrow minded in those times.

The next port was Dar es Salaam, and then we sailed on to Tanga. This was the East Africa run. I remember one night while we were anchored in a small bay in Tanga. It was a lovely, quiet evening I was leaning over the rail when suddenly, out leapt a massive giant manta ray. It must have been all of 10ft wide, and it made a mighty splash when it fell back into the water.

The boson (boatswain) and I went ashore in the little dinghy, as the port had no pier.

We went to the nearest bar, called the African Bar. Nearly all the bars were called the African Bar. The two of us played darts against two Indians, who had no idea how to play darts. Indians were quite wealthy in those days, and when they lost the game, the next round of drinks was on them.

The next port was Beira Portuguese East Africa, at this port there were loading quays. You had to wait your turn to be unloaded, it's known that ships can be there weeks at a time. They had a radio station called Radio Beira, and played music 24 hours a day. Then on to Durban, which was the best port that I liked. It was a very anglicized city. Natal, a province of South Africa, had a lot of leanings towards the U.K.

Apartheid was started in 1948 by the first South African President Milan, but our government turned a blind eye to what was going on.

The country was split into three races. The indigenous people - the blacks - were treated as third-rate citizens. The Cape Colour were second-rate citizens, and the whites who were in the minority were the top dogs. Both the Labour and the Conservative governments went along with the South African regime.

Pressure from the Wilson Labour government finally brought about change in that part of the world. It was said by Prime Minister Ian Smith of Rhodesia that it would not change in a thousand years. The British Labour government returned it back to a democratic government, but unfortunately it was later governed by Mugabe and renamed Zimbabwe. Robert Mugabe has now completely decimated the country with starvation and the sky-rocketing cost of living. The country's G.D.P is now out of hand. The farms are now fallow. The Zimbabweans took over the lands from the whites and the indigenous people forced the white farmers off their land. The biggest problem is that they could not manage properly; most farms are now a wilderness, where nothing is grown.

The people live in fear, and democracy is a joke in Zimbabwe, its capital now known as Harare. It is now a dictatorship under Mugabe. As I write this passage the top news is that Mugabe, after 30 years in power, has finally been defeated at the elections... but is still trying to hang on to power. Three weeks after the election, Mugabe will still not release the voting figures!

South Africa is now rid of apartheid, and is the most improved country in all Africa, but they still have problems, such as crime and AIDS. The biggest problem is that President Mbeki has not handled the AIDS disease, which is now endemic in the country, and he is saying there is no problem in the Zimbabwean government. Nelson Mandela was born too early; this is the man who had more respect than any other leader in the World, and after 30 years on Robin Island (gaol) he came out with much dignity, but age was against him.

Cape Town is a beautiful port, but to tie up in Cape Town is quite an event. The Cape is situated at the apex of Africa, where the Southern Atlantic and Indian Oceans meet. However, while tied up in Cape Town, there is always a massive swell running as the docks are not landlocked, they are open to the sea. They have to have about 20 ropes to secure the ship.

The back-drop of Capetown is a lovely sight, with Table Mountain, when the clouds descend on the mountain it looks like a huge table-cloth.

I left the *Wayfarer* when I got back to Liverpool, and signed on the *Successor*, a Harrison boat. The ship was an improvement on the Liberty ships built by the Americans during the war. We went up to Glasgow for deck cargo, which were locomotives bound for East Africa. The rest of the cargo would be taken on in Liverpool.

After the cargo was loaded, and lashed up and chocked off, we set sail from Glasgow and proceeded down the River Clyde. As soon we were clear of the Clyde we hit the Irish Sea. There was a big storm blowing up. With the ship having a heavy load on deck, we were top heavy and it felt like we could turn over at any time.

We hove to in Laxy Bay for three days, until the weather abated. From my experience, I can say that when the Irish Sea is angry, it can be the roughest sea in the world. At times the ship was rolling so badly that you had one foot on the deck and the other foot on the bulkhead (wall) of the cabin. You lay in your bunk, trying to get some sleep, while you felt the ship roll to 40 degrees. She would shudder and then come back again. After three days in Laxy Bay hoved to, we set sail again for Liverpool.

When I got back to Liverpool I had to see the shipping superintendent about the state of my mattress. It was not the right size, as it was a single mattress and my bunk was a double size. I could see by his attitude that he didn't seem to care. I told him if the ship started to roll, I would end up on the springs, but he just said it would be alright. I told him to stick his ship where 'Paddy stuck his ninepence'. I asked for my cards and left Harrison's for good.

I signed on the *Assyria*; Cunard also had the *Asia* and the *Arabia*. These were sister-ships and they were intermediate ships running to Montreal, Quebec and Two Rivers, a port where the river St Lawrence branches off.

The Chief Officer was a right prat. When he was sober he was OK, but when he had his lotion (gin) down him he could be a right bastard. He was a Royal Navy Reserve Lieutenant. I remembered the time when he was sober and asked me to come back, the next trip. I told him no way.

When we arrived in Montreal, he gave me orders to get my water hoses ready to take on fresh water. He couldn't understand that the water pressure is 65 ton-a-hour. Jimmy Quirk had told me, only use their hoses on the quay, as the ship's hoses would burst under the pressure in Montreal. Naturally I used the quay hoses and the tanks were filled in no time.

I went ashore to play some football against one of the Manchester liners and came back only to be summoned to the mate's room. He was pissed as a newt, gave me a right dressing down, he could not understand about the water hoses. On the next day he was pious as a punch, I had made a light gang-way, as there was a big rise and fall in the Montreal tides; the light gang-way made it easier for the watchman to move about.

He had the audacity to call me in his room for a drink, but the day before he had wanted to give me a bad discharge, also to prevent me being allowed to sail as a carpenter. He was a Jekyll and Hyde nut case. In fact he asked me to come back on the next trip, I told him, no way, as I am a relieving carpenter, as the other carpenter is only having a trip off.

Later, the shore superintendent, a man called Ginger Roscoe, said I was complimented and had good reports from the Chief Officer of the *Assyria*, believe it or not.

He explained to me that the procedure in Cunard was that you started your career on the smaller ships, then worked your way up to the larger vessels, eventually to the Queens (either *Mary* or *Elizabeth*). He asked me to start with the S.S. *Bothnia*.

I joined the *Bothnia* at the Canada coal tips. My heart sank when I set eyes on her. As she was a coal burner, the coal was stacked so high that you couldn't see the galley for coal. The ship was built in the twenties and the only fresh water was from a hand pump in the galley. Even the skipper had to have water brought up to his room in big jugs. The only place to eat was in your cabin. The cabin was very small, about eight feet by five. My room was right foreward. You had to wash in a bucket, as there was no running hot water. To have a bucket bath, you put the bucket on the galley stove to heat the water, and then had your bath on deck.

I did eleven trips on the *Bothnia* as the saying goes (one trip out, and one trip home), we went to some great places. We went to Genoa and all the coastal ports; Livorno, Naples, Sicily and the Lipari Isles in Italy. Then we sailed to Spain to Cartagena, and then on to Casablanca. This was the run with plenty of vino, or plonk to be had.

Casablanca had a large breakwater as you entered the port,

leaving the port was a pantomime. There was only one tug that heaved you out, and they had it down to a fine art. They steered you towards the breakwater, on which some small coastal craft were berthed, we then swung hard over. Normally, this would snap the bow rope. The tug would retrieve the snapped rope, and take it aboard their vessel for salvage.

What I will never forget is the beautiful entrance and harbour of Naples when we sailed into the bay at sunrise.

This would be in 1953, I saw large areas of desolation and poverty in Naples. The people of Naples literally lived like rats, below ground. Almost everywhere you saw, had been flattened by bombing during the war. This was what Mussolini's war had created.

This is the time I remembered in Naples. This was when England played Hungary at Wembley and the Hungarians annihilated England 6-3. The Italian dockers celebrated as if Italy had won the World Cup. That was the end of England's supremacy in world football. It was also the start of Italian and Spanish classical football.

I remember the time when I sailed with the S.S. *Bothnia* into Glasgow, as we sailed up the Clyde towards Glasgow we had to anchor off as we approached John Brown's shipyard and they were launching the Queen's yacht, *Britannia*. She looked great. Her hull was black, they must have used special paint as it gleamed in the sunlight.

This old rust bucket the *Bothnia* was a swine to take on fresh water. The fresh water tank air vents were badly designed and the breathing pipes were too small, which meant that when the tanks were being filled with water, the air couldn't get out of the tank, they kept blowing. You had to turn the water pressure down, until I found another way of releasing the air pressure in the tank.

There was a tap bolt on top of the tank manhole lid in the lazereet (a small rope locker at the stern end); I removed the bolt. A rush of air came out of the hole, which seemed to solve the problem. I went ashore for a couple of pints with the shore gang, before coming back later that night.

I was chatting with the watchman, I forgot all about the water. Suddenly remembering, I rushed aft, down to the lazereet. Much to my horror, I found it was half full of water, which was gushing out of where I had removed the stud-bolt. As we were leaving for Liverpool the next day to arrive on Christmas Eve, I didn't want us to be delayed, so I never mentioned the flood of water in the rope locker!

We arrived in the river at Liverpool, on Christmas eve.

The pilot came aboard, Cunard had their own pilots. Instead of waiting for the tide to make, as normally we would go into the Canada entrance to our berth at Canada no. 1, the pilot took the ship into the Prince's river entrance, where we locked in. I believe this had never been done before. We proceeded to Trafalgar, Brambly-More, Clarence, Nelson and Huskisson docks, and finally on to the Canada coal tip quay. It had taken us four hours to get from the Prince's entrance to the Canada coal tips, we tied up at 4am on Christmas morning. I was leaving the ship anyway, but the Chief Officer must have had a fit when he saw the water in the rope locker.

* * * * * * * * * * * * * *

My job at night going down the Suez Canal was to operate the big search light, on the (night head) or bow of the ship. It certainly lit up the way down the canal, and even today, as the canal is not lit up, ships use their own lighting. The Canal Authorities would rent you one of their searchlights. While we were at Port Suez, we called in for fresh water, which was delivered in huge barges. The Chief Officer called up one of the water barges over to our ship; the barge was manhandled by a large, moustached Egyptian. When he reached our ship and found out we only wanted 12 tons of water, he was enraged at the small amount of water. He wanted to throw the mate over the side.

On the canal there where bum boats selling their wares. One famous bum boat was an Arab who called himself Jock MacGregor. He sold everything, mostly crap, but he was entertaining. He dressed in a pinstriped suit and wore a homburger hat. He was just one of the characters of the canal.

I remember that during the British forced occupation of the Suez Canal, my ship being a *Harrison* boat meant the Scousers stationed on the canal knew it to be a Liverpool boat, and would give us a shout. They were probably homesick. Shortly afterwards the British were kicked out of Egypt.

I found it strange returning back up the canal. The barracks the British built were still out there, it was like a ghost town, not a soul in sight.

The other destinations we sailed to, while the Suez Canal was still blocked, were on the South African run. We picked up bunkers (oil) at Las Palmas, in the Canary Islands, and then went on to South Africa. These were great ports to go to.

Durban was a very modern city. I remember travelling on a rickshaw, but it must be said, that we the English went along with apartheid. I feel revulsion today that we supported the South African government, which was a totally undemocratic government. Thatcher, who came into office as the Tory Prime Minister in 1979, actually called Nelson Mandela a terrorist. Those words must stick in her throat today. She also believed that General Pinochet of Chile was a good leader; he was nothing but a dictator and a murderer.

The Americans sided with the right wing government of Vietnam. They went in gung ho, but they never realized that Ho-Chi-Minh was more than a match for the Americans, and after years of bloodshed, the Americans had to pull out after losing over 50,000 young men. There were more bombs dropped on Vietnam and Cambodia than all the bombs dropped in the 2nd world war. It took three Presidents to end it, but now Vietnam is a thriving holiday resort.

The Americans had interfered with Cuba, Chile and most of the South Americas, imposing their type of democracy on them. America does not like the word socialism   Unfortunately our country have contracts with these tyrants. The underdeveloped countries need help, yes, but unfortunately the third world is still being fleeced not only by the West, but China is now the new coloniser taking its share from the African continent. The Chinese are the modern colonizers.

The South African regime finally released one of the greatest leaders in the world, Nelson Mandela, who would have made one of the finest leaders the world has had. But sadly, the years of incarceration on Robin Island took their toll in the many years of lost leadership. He no doubt would have been a better leader than they have now in Mbeki. But Mandela laid the foundations to set South Africa on the road to being a democratic country, where whites and blacks would become equal citizens. This will not happen overnight, it will take time.

South Africa is the host country in 2010 during the World Cup year. This will certainly go a long way to moving progress.

The Three Caballeros, Galley boy, Tony, and me.
Somewhere in the Pacific, Frisco bound, 1953

#4 Hatch

*MV Athol Duke –
Pacific 1954
Stormy seas en route
to San Francisco*

*Angry seas in the Pacific,
approaching the
"International date line"*

CHAPTER TWENTY-SIX

Married To Eileen

I started courting Eileen in 1958; at the time I was secretary of Mount Carmel Men's CYMS Social Club. I knew Eileen's dad before I met her, because at that time I used to call to Billy and Mary's house for a cup of tea and a chat before I went home after the club closed. There was a priest at Mount Carmel called Father Joe Daley; he was a great man. We had two billiards teams and two bowls teams, and Father Joe was a member of the bowls team. We played at our home green at Prince's Park. Some of the other team members were also members of the Orange Lodge, and they took a liking to Father Joe. He was the first priest I knew to remove his dog collar and wear an open-necked shirt when not on official business.

I first met Eileen one day when she arrived home after a long cycle ride. She used to call me Mr. Stamper, which remains a standing joke today, when I'll say to her, "You used to have respect for me!" We still have a laugh about it. Mr. Stamper indeed... I fell in love with her. She makes things come alive, she always seemed happy, she is a very good communicator, nothing gets on top of her and everybody loves her.

I married Eileen on September 24th 1960, in Mount Carmel in High Park Street. We had our reception at Tramway Road Army Barracks.

After we got married, we went on our honeymoon to Dublin. It was the first time we had flown, a week later we returned back to Liverpool stony broke and we had to get the bus home, as we couldn't afford the taxi fare.

#4 Hatch

Left to right: Maria, Wilf and my mother, Me & Eileen, Billy and Mary, Eddy Maher my bestman.
Brides maids, Eileen Carr and Betty Carr.
Taken outside of Our Lady of Mount Carmel, High Park Street, September 24th 1960

End of an era: 18 Canova Street, where we spent very happy years watching the kids growing up. Two days later, after the picture was taken, the house was demolished, 1976

We were very lucky to rent a terrace house in Canova Street, Edge Hill, as it was very hard to get a rented house in those days. This was a good area to bring up the kids, and we had four children in five years. Our first born was Jacqueline, then Gerard, then Paul and finally the baby, Michelle. These years were the happiest times of our lives.

Eileen had all our children at home. I remember an hour before Jacqueline was born. Eileen wanted to go up to her mum's in Hough Green but I said, "I don't think so!" As soon as I said that, her waters broke, and having no phone I dashed up to Clint Road to the phone box. There were two young girls in the phone box; I was in so much of a hurry that I pulled them out of the phone box. An hour later, Jacqueline was born. Eileen never had many problems during her pregnancies, but when Jacqueline reached motherhood, unlike her mum, she had a very bad time of it in Whiston Hospital with her first born Samantha. Jacqueline gave birth to Aidan in the bathroom of her house; her mum delivered him. I was so proud of Eileen. She has a calming effect, and she does not panic.

We never had much as the children grew up. Eileen and I slept in the middle room with the four kids in the front room, in two double bunk beds. The back room was a bathroom, but we had no W.C or hand wash basin in the house, only the sink in the back kitchen. But we were lucky as there were not many houses in the street that even had a bathroom. The toilet was at the bottom of the backyard.

I remember when the children were young in Canova Street, during the dark winter nights, if Michelle wanted to go to the toilet, she had to have Paul escort her down the yard and sing a song to her. As it was very dark at bottom of the yard, she would do the same for him. With having four kids, our house always had lots of kids running in and out. I was fortunate in having a car, so we went out at the weekends. It was nothing for us if we had our four, plus at least two more kids who came along for the ride, but we had some fun.

While I was working at Cammell Lairds as a shipwright on submarines, I got Eileen's younger brother Billy Quinn a job, to be an apprentice shipwright. Billy was approaching the age of 16. I had a word with Joe, the Head Foreman shipwright. I spun him a yarn, using a bit of psychology saying that I had asked in the main office if they could start a young apprentice shipwright. I told Joe they had said, they had no vacancies, to which Joe replied that I shouldn't worry, Billy would start his apprenticeship. The bluff worked; he started on the Monday morning. I also got Billy into the joiners' union U.C.A.T.T. after he finished his time at Cammell Laird's. Billy Quinn is now turned 60 and living in South Africa. He has a grown up family; he's a granddad now. How time flies!

I was the Clint Road residents' chairman or representative, as we were in the middle of the general purchase of the properties. One time I had a strange delegation that came to my house, there was about twenty mothers of the children who went to Edge Hill Boys' School. The nub of the trouble was it was alleged that a young mother, who lived opposite the school in our street, was inviting young boys into her house after school. She had a drinking problem, but it was obvious what was happening.

I had the sad task of tackling the problem. I went through the official channels. As the mother had four children of her own, it was obvious that her children would be at risk, and her children could be taken into care. This was a sad conclusion. I had to remark to the Chief Inspector that if a man was found to be taking young girls into his house, his feet wouldn't touch the floor. I find that to be no different to this case where a woman was inviting young boys in. I am glad to say that things worked out well for the children and they were fostered out. I saw two of them some time later; they looked fine and were well-mannered and clean.

But there was a time when my wife found the children in the filthy back-entry. She took them in and bathed them, then she found them some of our kids' cast-offs. Their mother was always asking me to rush them to the Children's Hospital in Myrtle Street, when they had swallowed something they shouldn't have.

Eileen worked for the Provident (the Provy) as a collector. I didn't like the job because I felt it was dangerous as she was mugged twice, so I told her to pack the job in. The next time, it could be serious. Eileen has a very strong will, but she finally gave up the job. She didn't have it easy with four kids, all of them young. I can see her now, with the pram taking the kids to school; the pram was a useful transport vehicle while the children were in school. She would take the washing once a week in the same pram, up to the wash-house in Kensington, then get back home, pick up the kids from school, give them their lunches, take them back up to school, and finally pick them up again at 3:30.

This would go on five days a week, as Eileen was still at the Provy, she only worked when the kids were at school. When the school holidays came round, Eileen had to keep her eye out for the kids and she would be getting my evening meal ready. She just got on with it. It was nothing for Eileen to push two kids from Edge Hill to her mother's in the Dingle (we only had Jacqueline and Gerard then), and then she would have to push them back home in time to get my evening meal ready when I got home.

In the early days before the car, I went to work on my bike. We were happy for most of the time. No babysitters for Eileen, my job every night was the polishing of four pairs of shoes. I would be up 6:30am to make up the fire, which was our only means of heating. I had left for work before Eileen and the kids were up, but I made sure they got up to a nice, warm fire.

I bought my first car from Palace Motors in Birkenhead for £350. It was a Hillman 1600cc and it was held together with fibreglass; it was a load of rubbish. It looked alright to me, but you find out the hard way. After the Hillman, I bought an Austin Cambridge, another banger, but she was a good runner. Then I bought a better car, it was an Austin Maxi 1600cc hatchback. I look back fondly at the Maxi and the personalities that the car taxied, including Michael Foot (the leader of the Labour Party), Barbara Castle (the transport minister), Peter Shaw (another Labour minister), the Catholic Archbishop Torello (the bishop for social justice in the free world) and Bishop Warlock (who eventually became Liverpool's Archbishop). The only trouble I had with the Maxi, was that the gear stick would always come out of the floor. I had to stick it back in the housing.

I remember a time when Father Joe Howell of St Anne's asked me if I would take the girls from St Anne's youth club to North Wales. They had an old Morris Commercial second hand ambulance, and there were 20 young girls. Eileen and our four kids came aboard too. You had to double the clutch when you changed gear, but we got there and back again five days later in one piece. It was great fun. Joe Howell has long left the priesthood and is a happily married with a family. He lives over the water in the Wirral.

At that time, Eileen and I were involved with an organization called F.S.A (Family Social Action). During the summer months the group would organize an outing to Frith Beach in north Wales for people in the parish, no matter what their religion. We hired two double decker buses to get there. Our group would organize fun for the kids. We had the usual sack races, and everyone got a prize. Everybody had a good time. I look back at those times, and I feel that we were putting something good in their lives. Most of the families couldn't afford holidays. There was Father Joe Howell, Tom and Anne Casey, Gerry Tweedle, Phil McAllaster,

And our wives gave great assistance in the organising the games, and the food, I think it went down very well, most could not afford a holiday.

CHAPTER TWENTY-SEVEN

Politics

I was very political in the sixties. I had a surgery in Dean Road every Saturday morning, although I was not an elected councillor, I was on the Borough Council, which was disbanded in the late seventies. There were two of us who had a surgery; one was the well known councillor and solicitor, Sir Harry Livermore. If there were legal problems, Harry would come to my aid.

The strangest request we both had was an Irish guy that came along to the surgery. He had his wife and six kids and told me that his house in Belfast had been machine gunned and he feared for their lives. I believed him to be a member of the U.V.F. His request was for us to find them some accommodation. This was Saturday morning, but we rang up Knowsley Council, and after a few hours search, finally we did get them fixed up.

During this time I was standing for council, my campaign was a well organized campaign and Bob Waring was my agent. At this time, the Liberals were steeply entrenched in Kensington. Although we still had a Labour M.P., Sir Arthur Irvine, he was a rubbish M.P. who had been elected on the back of the Attlee Government in 1945. I was the branch president in my union branch and I put in a resolution stating that he should retire from office as the M.P. for the Edge Hill constituency. Harry Livermore showed me the letter he sent to him, and there was no malice in the letter. Harry was asking him to go with some dignity left in him. He stood down at the next election, but we lost the seat to David Alton of the Liberal party, after 32 years of control. The Labour majority of 7,000 turned into a Labour deficit of 7,000.

Mike Black, Lord Mayor of Liverpool. I knew Mike as a old friend. Note the buses in the background, they are taking the victorious Liverpool team on a trip around the City. Mike supported Everton.

Bob Waring was the Labour candidate in that election. The Liberals were known for their pavement politics; Hughie Carr called them political prostitutes. Bob Waring fought for the seat in West Derby and finally won it in 1983. Bob was not selected this year; I think Bob is now past his sell-by date. Surely at the age of 78, he has to make room for a younger man.

I stood three times in Kensington, but lost every time. The people saw no wrong in the Liberal Party. The first time I lost by 24 votes. I had done quite well, and still lost, but I know I was the best candidate. I had a surgery every Saturday morning, lived in the area and knew the problems. The Liberal who won the seat was a 21 years old; he was still wet behind the ears. He was a poor councillor, who seemed to vanish after he was elected. A ruse the Liberals had during the elections, was to dump an old mattress in the back entry. People would complain. The Liberals had a piece of rope tied to the mattress, so they could then drag it down to another back entry. These are the stunts they got up to! The leader of the Liberal Democrats was a Sir Trevor Jones, who one year underspent from the rate support grant by £10 million. What this meant was, that the city was penalized a further £10 million so Liverpool had a total cut of £20 million. We only got £80 million instead of £100 million!

CHAPTER TWENTY-EIGHT

I Become a Joiner

In the winter of 1963, I was working on the river, closing the Herculaneum Dock. We had to wear life belts while we were working on a small stage hung over the quay wall, a matter of a foot from the river. There were big ice floes on the Mersey. I can remember when this winter first started. It began on Boxing Day, 1962. The football season was curtailed for 12 weeks and the pitches were like concrete. I read an article of why this intense weather came about, it stated that a very cold blanket of air was coming from Siberia, while a hot belt of air came up the Gulf Stream. These two belts of air met over this part of Europe and the hot air rose above the cold air. This kept us in an Arctic state, which carried on till April.

Throughout the winter we were working on the Brunswick River entrance gates, which had been badly damaged by a German coaster *Norderau*. The ship had accidentally rammed the huge 220 ton gates and there was a 15 foot twist in the gates.

The gates were taken from the river entrance by the Atlas floating crane in a upright position to the Queen's Dry Dock, where we repaired them. The water was pumped out of the dry dock. As the gates started to settle on the dock blocks, the pumping stopped, leaving about 15ft of water. Steel cables were stretched to the opposite side of the dock, taken to the capstan and were used to literally heave the gate until it toppled over, flat side to the dry dock floor, cushioned by the water in the dock. The dock was then emptied of water. This done, we could carry on repairing the gates. It took nine months, and was heavy, hard work. The sphinx must have been a cakewalk to erect, compared to this!

The gates were made of greenheart. We removed the massive heel post, which had to be renewed. Over the wintertime, the old heel post was cut up every night. We used the off cuts for cock wood (firewood). This was very good timber for your fire at home. It was cut into eight-inch segments, two foot thick, with a two man crosscut saw. It would take about half an hour to cut each segment.

We had some strange jobs, working for the Dock Board. On one job, we had to inspect the Brunswick and Harrington entrance gate chains. The opening and closing chains lay at the bottom of the dock. The method we used was known as the limpet box, which was 30 by 6 by 6 feet and looked like a barge, but opened at one end. It was lifted on end and lowered into the right position. The gunnels, or the edges of the limpet had hemp or sisal fastened to them. This stopped any leaks getting into the limpet after the water had been pumped out. The limpet was fastened to the quay, and two heavy electric water pumps were lowered into the limpet to remove the water. As the water was being pumped out, the pressure of water on the outside pressed the limpet to the quay. When the water was removed you climbed down the ladder, and then you could work below the water line.

One Saturday morning, our task was to tighten the huge nuts to the dock gates. The spanner was very heavy, and it took two of us to lift it. The hammer we used was called a munday hammer. To get to the job, we used a small painter, or row boat. I became proficient at sculling, which means using one oar at the stern of the boat, making a figure of eight with the blade of the oar.

After nine months work on these gates, they were taken out of the dry dock, and transported one at a time back to the Brunswick river entrance. Before the gates were put back into place, a diver would go underwater, and use a powerful water cannon to clear away the mud away from the gate area. Where the gates were to be fitted on the bed of the river there was a granite shaped dish, and very large solid iron ball weighing a ton was lowered into place, the heel of the gate likewise had a housing for this iron ball. This allowed the gate, when fixed in position, to swivel backwards and forwards. Linking the gates to the wall were iron collar straps fastened to the wall.

The work for the Dock Board was very heavy work. I remember in 1963, when we had the worst smog recorded, visibility was about one yard and every means of transport was cancelled. I had to walk home from the Herculaneum Dock, and it took me about two hours to get home. At that time thousands of old people died of lung disease, and it was at this time the government brought out the Smokeless Fuel Act. What must be said it worked. I don't think we have had any smog to complain about since. In most cases the tram car was a safer mode of transport, than buses, as during the time of the great smog of 1963, buses were running up on the sidewalks. As I said, the year 1963 was also bad for the big freeze-up, there were ice floes on the Mersey.

As most houses used coal for heating, deliveries were hard to come by; we had to go to the railway coal yards to get a half hundred weight of coal. The government then gave out massive contracts to make sure that the gas fires and boiler heaters were modified and would be using natural gas, and not coal gas. There were far more people went on to gas heating. Central heating was no more a luxury. I didn't have central heating till 1976, I had lived in six houses in my lifetime, none with central heating.

As my children were growing up, I decided to move on from being a shipwright. The work had declined as there was no shipping in the south end area of the docks. The Amalgamated Society of Woodworkers (A.S.W.) would accept shipwrights. The old A.S.W sadly became the Union Construction and Allied

Trade and Technicians (U.C.A.T.T.). I joined the Liverpool 2nd branch, in Ullet Road. I later became branch President, with Frank Foley as the secretary and Aleck Smyth as the treasurer. I held that position for 19 years.

Being the branch President I would invite speakers along to the branch meetings to make the meetings more interesting, visitors such as Lady Margaret Simey, Leader of the Council John Hamilton, Professor John Ashton, and Eddy Sabino, a man who represented an Electrical Union. I thought it brought some spice to the normal humdrum union meeting

My first job as a joiner was working for J.B Edward's in 1964, they were the contractors for I.C.I at Runcorn.

Being an ex-shipwright, I had to adapt to joiners' work. At the time I started, there were only 12 joiners working on the site. I found out that the men had no shop steward. Nobody to represent them, it seemed they were not interested. I convened a short meeting, where I was duly elected as the shop steward. A shop steward was needed, as the site at Runcorn had a very large area.

As the work progressed, many more joiners started, till we had almost 120 joiners working on the site. This made my responsibility much greater, I had to have a deputy shop steward elected, as my work load was growing. Sometimes, it would take me two days to visit all the joiners on site. On one occasion I found out that the contractor had started a joiner, who had no union card, I then had to escort the man to the works office, where I played merry hell with the agent. I had already made it known to the agent, that if he was to start a joiner, I had to see his union card; unfortunately this man didn't have a union card. The poor bugger came from the north east, so unfortunately he had return back home to get a joiners' union card. I played hell with the agent, but I am glad to say the man returned to the site with his union card, as he realized that this area was a solid union area.

One of my mates was Roy Trafford who happened to be a mate of Ritchie Starkey (Ringo Star); he used to go down to Ringo's house down south. Roy is a private person, but through Ringo, he got to know the likes of McCartney, Lennon and all the show business people. Roy still kept his privacy, but he did show us some photographs, when he was down at Ringo's place at Wadebridge.

I remember a time when the whole site decided to put in a claim for overall site condition money of two shillings an hour, as there were different condition moneys paid in every part of the plant. The conditions varied on the site, we thought a higher payment should be made. The whole site amalgamated to ask for a better site condition money. This was turned down by our relevant unions. The union would not take on the I.C.I.

We took this dispute back to the men on the site and convened a meeting. We informed then what had taken place between the officials and the I.C.I, and that the company had refused our case. We then put a vote to the men if we should proceed to strike, but the men decided to go back to work.

Some months later when I finished with J.B Edwards, Billy Heaps, who was my labourer who had worked with me, came to me and asked if I wanted to do a foreigner (job on the side). He had got a job as a deck hand on a German E-Boat, running contraband around the Mediterranean area and needed us to do some modifications to the boat. My mate Les Booth and I, built chocks for two large fresh water tanks, we opened up the foredeck and cut out a small hatch, we then caulked the deck. I asked Billy to get some black marine pitch, he came back with black ordinary street pitch (of which I think he had knocked it off, to save buying it) he said it would be OK! We got our pay and the best of luck to Billy, as there must have been a right mess when the pitch melted in the hot Mediterranean sun!

While working at the I.C.I I remember a terrible tragedy, that happened in the cooling room on the site. On top of this building there were four large fans with a 15 foot diameter span. The I.C.I. Deputy Head of Construction was viewing the job up on top of a ladder. As he looked over the top of the fan room, it was alleged that some electrician was supposed to switch on the pump, but the wiring was wrong and the fan came on instead of the pump. The fan's huge blades spun around, catching this poor unfortunate man; his head smashed the carbon blades of the fan. A team of medics got him down off the building and his head was covered in heavy bandaging. The doctor attending him looked so shocked, his face was white. The injured man was a big strong man, a smaller man would have died probably much quicker, but he died three days later. It's a known fact that there are more fatalities in the construction industry than in any other industry.

After three years with J.B Edwards, we were all made redundant. I worked for a short time on the Liverpool Playhouse extension for Tysons, where we had a young chargehand joiner. My mate and I requested that he bring us a section of shuttering for a beam section which we were setting up. The next minute we heard a mighty yell. The chargehand had been removing a temporary cover, which was part of the shuttering from an opening in the floor, when he fell 30ft through the opening onto some scaffolding boards, which slightly cushioned his fall. However, the poor man broke his back. Rather than receiving compensation, the firm guaranteed him a job for life. I told him he was a bloody fool for accepting it, as he had a very good chance of receiving compensation. Tysons is now, no longer in business! I had heard that Les Tyson was quite a character. He once had an argument with a labourer, and the labourer wanted to have a fight with Les. They went to the back of the site, where Les flattened the guy. Les Tyson was a hard nut.

Tyson's firm is finished now; they went into liquidation. This was the firm who done some of the finest work in Liverpool. One of their most successful jobs was India Buildings, which was badly bombed during the war. Sadly Tyson's is no more.

My mate and I then moved on to the shopping precinct at Clayton Square and worked for Trollope and Colls. The pay at Tyson's had been rubbish, and we literally moved next door. Incidentally, Trollope and Colls is the oldest construction company in Liverpool, they were building the new shopping precinct in the old market of St John's. This job cost three lives due to an earlier incident on Elliot Street, when workers were positioning a large concrete beam, which toppled on top of them. The bonus was very poor here too.

After two years, we were again made redundant. It was at the start of the building of the shopping precinct that I thought was most interesting as Queens Square was a thriving place, with the wonderful smell of the fruit market, and at the opposite end of the square was the Stork Hotel which was quite a busy hotel.

Some of our scaffolding came to the side of the wall of the Royal Court Theatre. During the afternoon periods we would sneak into the rear of the Theatre, and watch the rehearsals.

CHAPTER TWENTY-NINE

Working on the Teaching Hospital

After a short time, in 1968 I got a job on the new Liverpool Teaching Hospital. This job was one of the happiest I had in the building industry, it lasted for ten years. The hospital was being built for the North West Regional Health Authority. Each firm put in a tender to build the Hospital. Tearson's, with a bid of £11 million, was successful, which was far less than MacAlpines bid of £14 million. But after only a year, they were removed, as they could not handle the enormity of the task. The financiers were B.I.C.C (British Insulated Calendar Cables), another firm which is no more.

MacAlpines then accepted the contract. "On Time and Material" a contract that they couldn't lose, as in effect, the longer the job went on, the more money they made. As the old saying goes, "More days, more dollars,"

But after five years, the B.I.C.C. were in the red to the tune of £10 million.

MacAlpines stayed on as a caretaker to the site, till they brought in Bovis Construction Company.

Had Bovis been the first contractor, the hospital would probably have been completed three years earlier because of their know-how. MacAlpines just milked the job. When Bovis came on the site, the first item on their agenda was to give the workers better facilities and canteens. They had all the old huts demolished, and replaced them with new and better huts. No more sitting on long forms, eight men per table. We were given square tables and chairs, four men to a table, and proper washing facilities, even salt and pepper on the table. Bovis transformed the site, putting back some dignity, which was owed to us. This is why they call MacAlpines a ladder and hand-cart firm. I was the sick steward (no it didn't mean I was sick all the time). Every Thursday I would collect 2/6d off each man, so when somebody was off sick they would get a small payment in-lieu. Having a sick steward gave everyone a sense of belonging and security.

Bovis was brought in because the North West Regional Health Authority had already lost millions of pounds on the contract. What must be said is that they still got the hospital cheap at £45 million; this was even stated by one of the architects. It is a very large hospital, but I recently heard it is to be made into a smaller, more compact hospital. We will have to see!

It was a good place to work, not because of money or wages, but as it had a friendly disposition about the place. There was always something going on. I must say, it was the happiest job that I have had. It was not the money that was good about the job, but the camaraderie. The man who drove the centre crane, who was known as the Gypsy, had loudspeakers rigged up, that came along the jib of the crane, playing out music to one and all.

I mentioned before of the fatalities in the construction industry, but I am proud to say that on this job, there was not one fatality in the 11 years of construction.

But what has to be said is that there are more deaths in the building industry than there are in the mines and on the docks put together. Some of the so-called building companies cut corners, regarding safety. The fatal figures one year alone stood at 160 deaths through bad safety conditions. This is because there are not enough government inspectors, It is a fact, that Thatcher reduced factory inspectors during her 10 year reign.

Jack Stamper

CHAPTER THIRTY

Shrewsbury Trials

It must have been disturbing for the citizens of Shrewsbury, when the court trials of 1973 were being staged. The police outnumbered the protesters in Shrewsbury, and 24 members were convicted of which 6 were imprisoned. Two of the six were Des Warren and Ricky Tomlinson, Des received 3 years and Ricky got 2 years, charged under the 1878 Act of Conspiracy. During their years in gaol, the two prisoners refused to wear prison garb, in fact they never wore any clothes at all and went on a dirty strike; they defecated on the prison walls and floor, then they both decided to go on hunger strike.

After several weeks, Des Warren had a prison visit from my fellow shop steward friends Alan Abrahams and Billy Jones, of whom I had worked with some years ago as a shipwright. They then visited Ricky Tomlinson and related to Ricky that Des couldn't last out the hunger strike as he was failing fast. Alan Abrahams said "Only you, Rick, can save Des, by coming off the hunger strike." Ricky knew what to do and sent a message to Des saying that they had done enough, short of killing ourselves, and that they should call it a day, Des was angry and saddened, he thought Ricky had double crossed him. After all, they had made a pact. Des never spoke to Ricky for years, but unfortunately Ricky could never tell him what had transpired at the visit of Alan Abrahams, but after many years Des Warren found out what had transpired between them and they became good friends again.

This story was all about people who have been dealt wrongly

and dehumanised by the state, what lengths men will go to, to stand up for their rights, and to go further, to show the public in the domain how far an evil government will go. Read Des Warren's book "The Key to my Cell". Des tells of the many gaols he had to endure. In one prison he went to he was met by a horrible warden, whose first words to Des, making sure the other inmates heard, were, "That will teach you a lesson, not to play with little girls." These are the things he had to put up with.

The defendants where found guilty of the ancient Law of the "1878 Act of Conspiracy". It was the heinous sentence the Judge dealt out which shocked the court and even the Chief Constable of Shrewsbury. The footnote is two of the jurors ran out of the court and the judge ordered them back into the court. The jurors where deeply shocked at the severity of the sentence and they were given wrong information in the jury room. It had been alleged that the court official actually went into the jury room and advised them that the defendants, if found guilty, would only pay a small fine at the most, his action surely was illegal. The whole trial was a farce, brought about by the Thatcher government to break the unions. And furthermore, it was a Labour government who came into power after the Heath government and actually kept the men in gaol. Roy Jenkins, who was the Home secretary, would not discuss the case.

They still will not release the secret documents of the Shrewsbury trials after more than thirty-eight years.

I still see an old mate of mine called Peter Melvin, from the Teaching Hospital site. He reminded me of the time when he started at the Teaching Hospital. He had to finish off his apprenticeship as the firm he previously worked for went broke and he was a little bit overawed at the size of the job. I hopefully put him at ease, telling him that they were a great bunch of lads, he would get used to things and everything would be fine. I found it nice of him, to remember many years later, my little chat to him.

During the construction I had two lucky escapes. The first one happened when I had to go up on the scaffolding one day to retrieve a long pinch bar, and it was raining very heavily. I was up on the 12th floor and as I stepped on to the scaffolding board it twisted. I found myself on my back and nearly fell off the scaffolding, but I hung on. As the weather was so foul there was not a single person about. I had broken my ankle and had to crawl off the scaffolding. Then Les, my workmate, got me to the hospital. My union solicitor was more than useless, as although the scaffolding was badly fitted, all I received was my loss of earnings. I don't think the solicitor gave good advice due to the strong evidence that the scaffolding was badly fitted.

My second skirmish on the scaffolding was again on top of the building. I bent down to pick up my hammer and my arse bumped on a staging pole, which propelled me forward. This time, I grabbed onto the upright pole to keep from falling off.

When we were building the hospital we had bad press, which was an insult to our integrity. The press accused us of always being on strike, but this was totally untrue. The only time that we were on strike was the 10 week official strike called by the union in 1972, which was about getting a wage rise. This was necessary as we were so poorly paid, you would have to rely on overtime to supplement your pay.

During the official builders' strike there were always some other little outfits which would scab it. Therefore, our site members would go out to the Merseyside area and persuade other outfits to stop their jobs. I and many others were called Flying Pickets, something I am proud of. This would be anyone who had a car, who could get round the sites quickly, to urge the men who were still working to come and join us. The car was vital to get round the area. There is always a stigma to being called a flying picket, but I was proud to be one. When we won the pay rise, the scabs got their increase in their wage packet also.

The strike culminated in the trial of the Shrewsbury Three, as mentioned earlier in this chapter.

I remember going on the demonstrations to support them. They were charged with contravening the 1878 Act by having an unlawful meeting or assembly. This is a pernicious act which belongs to the dark ages. As Ricky would say, "My arse" to that out dated piece of shit! I don't think the locals knew what hit them, with us marching up and down the High Street in Shrewsbury, as it was only a simple, little market town. One of the who were on trial was Ricky Tomlinson, now a nationally known comedian.

Denis Warren was one of the others sentenced, and this was the undoing of Denis' health, as he was made to do the full three years because he maintained he was not guilty. If Denis had agreed with the court's decision he would have out after 12 months goal. He died some years later because of what society had done to him. To think this all came about by urging the scabs to stop work, as it was an official strike.

The other defendant was John Llewach. I met him after the trial and he told me the tale. His brief was Sir Arthur Irvine Q.C.M.P for the Edge Hill Constituency. He asked him to plead guilty to the 1878 Act as he would get him off with a lighter sentence. John's words, not mine, were, "Fuck off" and he sacked him as his defending solicitor.

Irvine had told the constituency meeting of Edge Hill, some weeks earlier than the trial, that the law of conspiracy in the 1878 Act in the statute book must be eradicated and written out.

I confronted the MP about what he had said at the previous meeting, about getting rid of the law of conspiracy. He tried to deny what he had said to John Llewach, but I never believed Irvine's explanation. Afterwards I proposed to my union and Labour party branch that the Kensington Branch requested Sir Arthur Irvine to retire from the seat of Edge Hill, and he eventually stepped down.

I remember one of the many demonstrations I attended at the pier head. One was "The Right to Work March". This was the famous march to London. Incidentally my brother-in-law Chris Quinn also took part in the march, which echoed the famous 1935 Jarrow March. At the meeting, there in the crowd was Archbishop Warlock, who I knew quite well. A man next to me said "Is that the Archbishop standing there?" I said yes, and he replied, "Why doesn't he get up there and say something?" I told him that this morning at St Nicholas, the Archbishop had told the congregation that Christ would have joined the marchers in their cause. If that speech had been made nationally it would have had more impact than all the rhetoric that was spoken from the platform. On the platform were Eric Heffer, Bob Waring, Eddy Loyden and others. There were 20,000 plus to see the march off to London.

I had been introduced to the Archbishop some years earlier. He was, at that time, the Bishop of Portsmouth and never dreamt he would become the Archbishop of Liverpool. He told me an amazing tale about the time they were burying Archbishop Downey in the crypt of the cathedral. He was a young cleric at the time, and he noticed there were some of the locals who were looking very sad at the occasion. He said to me he thought, why all this sadness? While his family were looking to see what was in the Archbishop's house in Green Lane, they found the Archbishop had left £53000 to his kin, and not a penny to charity or the church.

A friend of mine Tom Casey, who had known Archbishop Warlock, had introduced me to him. Tom was not a motorist and I had a car, so Tom asked me if I could ferry them around the area where he wanted to go. It was alright by me. I also had the privilege to be in the company of Bishop Sheppard. We used to have interdenominational talks and spent some great meetings at Tom Casey's house in Fairfield Street. I am glad to see that they put up a memorial to both Bishops in Hope Street. This took place in 2008, the Capital of Culture year.

The hospital site was very handy for me. As I lived in Edge Hill, it only took me about five minutes to get to work. During the summer, working on top of the hospital, there was a fantastic view. You could see Blackpool Tower, and on a clear day you could pick out the Cumberland Hills across Morecambe Bay. During the time I was working at the hospital site, we moved to Booker Avenue in January, 1976. We have enjoyed living there ever since. I like to look after my garden, and Eileen is a good help with that, as I can't get down to the weeds now. Eileen gets down and does it with no complaints. I go to Garston baths every day if I can; there is a group of us called the solv-ite gang, because we're always stuck against the wall, putting the world to rights. We're all reaching our eighties, some are much more. I am a mere youngster at 79, and I still have my hair!

During the Thatcher years there was an offshoot of the Tory party, an organisation called the Economic League. It was alleged that they made lists of names from men or women who would stand up for their rights, and put them in a book to be supplied to employers. These people would be black listed from attaining any work. This had gone on for many years.

I will give an example. A man I know by the name of Frank Foley was a shop steward, working for Morrison's the Builders in Pall Mall. The manager was visiting the site along with the site architect. The architect spotted Frank, and asked Mr Morrison, "Is that Mr Foley I see?" He ordered Mr Morrison to remove Frank off the site. Mr Morrison told Frank the news, and said to Frank if he did not remove himself from the site the firm would be in trouble. Frank, being a decent man of principles, removed himself from the site, instead of creating any bother and causing men to lose money from a strike.

Frank and the delegate went down to read up on the rules at the Central Library, and indeed there was passage in the architect rulings, this can happen. I suppose it was written in the 19th century. But the Labour Government outlawed this the piece of legislation, and not before time. In other words, no one can refer to the so-called Black List.

Frank knew this related to his time at the building of the Ford site, where Frank was the senior shop steward. This was the debt you received when you fought for your rights.

CHAPTER THIRTY-ONE

Family Life

When I lived in Edge Hill, my two youngest children were still at the local elementary school, Sacred Heart in Hall Lane. We had moved up to Booker Avenue and I was still working at the hospital site, which was near to Hall Lane. I would pick up Paul and Michelle at school to take them home. Eventually Paul went to Gerard's school at St Francis Xavier's, Woolton, and Michelle followed Jacqueline to Notre Dame in Woolton.

As a family, the weekends were spent in the car going to Wales, or up to the lakes, as the traffic was not as bad as it is today. I remember one time we were heading south on the M6 with the four kids in the back; there was no law about seat belts then. I was enjoying the ride, when Paul from the back piped up and started calling me, "Dad! Dad!"

I was concentrating on the road ahead but replied, "What do you want?"

Paul replied, "Errrr, the wheel has come off the trailer."

I looked in my mirror and to my horror I spotted the trailer wheel going a good steady 60 mph on its own. Luckily for us it didn't hit another vehicle but bounced back on to the hard shoulder. The trailer looked sad lying at an angle. When we jacked it up to put the wheel back on, I could only find two nuts. We took a chance and tightened the two nuts, and made it until the next service station. I bought this trailer cheap, but I didn't know the chassis was off a mini car. This meant that the axle was a split axle, and the only way the wheels kept together was pure luck. But we got to the camping site!

Our tent always looked like a bag of rags when it was erected; I don't think we were very good at camping. Anyway, we had good fun and many adventures camping.

On the way home, I decided to go up the A43. We got as far as Whitchurch, which is 73 miles from Liverpool, and the wheel shaft parted just outside a farmhouse. The farmer let me leave it in the yard till the next day, where I picked it up, and put it on a low loader. That was the end of camping.

We went to the Isle of Man, to my mother's house, mostly while she went away on her holidays. I can remember when Paul was about three years of age he always looked a bonny kid and was very blonde. One day he had his little sailor hat on, and not a stitch on him, and was trotting along Douglas promenade! That's what I call having no inhibitions.

There was an air of uneasiness at my mother's. Her biggest problem was that she consistently lived in the past. My mother was always running people down; it was always the other person in the wrong. My stepdad Wilfy had a right time with her; she was constantly nagging him, she gave him a dog's life. I accepted Wilfy as a good person and from what I saw, she constantly ridiculed him, but at times the picture wasn't all that bad. I remember Wilfy was a fisherman and he worked on a small drifter, fishing the Irish Sea. There were times when he and the crew would fish from early morning till evening, get back in the harbor at Douglas with a catch, but would have to let the fish go to feed the pigs because they couldn't sell it, or they missed the auction, and because there was no refrigeration on the island to keep the fish fresh, The pig swill would go some way to pay for the diesel, to get to and come back from the fishing grounds.

My eldest daughter Jacqueline said Granddad Wilfy dressed the best crab she ever tasted. He was very good with the children, even though they were not his grandchildren, but step-grandchildren. He truly treated them like his own, and the kids loved him. Unfortunately my mother could not share her love regarding including her own grandchildren. Gerard is a very loving child, but my mother seemed not to notice him. He was the quiet one. She remarked that Gerard was a Stamper. As my mother hated the Stampers, her problem was that Gerard looked like my father. Fortunately, Eileen's parents had the right attitude as grandparents. Billy and Mary were easy going, and we often went up to Eileen's parents' house on a Sunday. They would never show any favouritism with the grandchildren.

Quite often Billy and Mary spent their holidays with us. We went to Butlin's or the Isle of Man with them, and we had some great times.

I remember Wilfy telling me a tale about ashes. A solicitor visited the fishing boat Wilf fished on, and requested that they take with them a small, polished box of some person's ashes, and while they were at sea, they were to disperse them on the water. They would get £20 pounds for doing so. They agreed to do it, and all they thought about was the £20 notes as he handed the box to him, and they set sail. After some miles they set their nets, then after a couple of hours someone remembered the box. But after they got the box on deck, they couldn't figure out how to get the sodding box open. Johnny Kinnish got a hammer and smashed the box open, then threw the ashes on the water, saying to the poor departed man, "You can have the box as well," as he threw the casket into the sea.

When the boat got back to Douglas, the solicitor was waiting for them. He asked for the casket, and when they told the solicitor what had happened, he looked at them with disgust saying, "You silly bastards, there was a paper pullback on the bottom, so you could empty the contents. The casket was worth a few bob!" He strode off saying, "There will no more laying ashes on the sea by you gobshites."

The Isle of Man in the forties and fifties did a roaring trade in tourism, because going abroad was out of the question in those times. There would be a queue stretching the length of the Riverside Parade and bending back to the end of the floating roadway. Boat after boat would be available and to some people, the Isle of Man was going abroad. My mate Chris White and I regularly went to the Isle of Man in the forties. Chris met his wife Hilary there; she came from Crewe. Chris died this year, but they had 50 years of marriage and I know they were a happy couple. Eileen and I went down to their house in Crewe, the year before Chris died.

CHAPTER THIRTY-TWO

Knowsley Council

At the time I became unemployed from the Teaching Hospital, things where not too good on the job front. I got a job in Knowsley Council. I started in the Prescot depot. After working there for 9 months we set up a depot in Halewood, which made a lot of sense, as the workforce had to travel every day to Halewood to do the repairs on the council properties.

I became the joiners' foreman, and we had a good gang of lads at our depot. Christmas time was a time to unwind, and our depot was always the top depot to put on a party. Jim Corner got involved with the celebrations. He was the depot's Superintendent, but at Christmas time he was one of the lads. Ken Griffin, Jim's deputy, joined in as well. I had the use of the council van, so I went home every day for my dinner. No one was the wiser; it only took only ten minutes to get home.

One time I took it home for the weekend, when I had a little errand to do. Gerard, my eldest son, was employed by the North Yorkshire council. He had a motorbike, which was not ready for the road, and he was trying to get the bike to Liverpool. I used my own petrol I hasten to had, but I then used the van to bring the motor bike back to Liverpool, and put it in my garage. I rewound the milometer on the van to what it was on the Friday I borrowed it, so no one was any the wiser that I used the council van.

I had some problems with some tenants. One of my jobs was to visit the tenants, and during a visit to one house, the tenant said that the door handle had come off. I was quite annoyed when I saw the complaint, because the man of the house was obviously just too bloody lazy to fix it himself, and I told him so myself; it only needed four screws. They thought that the council had a never-ending budget, but with all the paper work it entailed, it would have cost about £30 to order it be fixed. Then I noticed the tenant's son, who was about 12 years old, was at home and it was a school day. I asked him, "No school today, son?"

I couldn't believe it when his mother said, "I sent him for ciggys."

I could not resist saying to his mum, "You are denying him his education, keeping him off school," but it fell on deaf ears.

There were times I had to tell some tenants to clean up their house before I would send the workmen in to do the repairs; some houses were not fit for pigs to live in.

There was one elderly man living on his own, in Torrance Drive, who was an invalid in a wheelchair. Unfortunately, his flat was filthy dirty. In the early hours one morning, the police noticed his front window broken and thought the property was vacant. The police had the house completely boarded up. Unfortunately, the problem was that the tenant was still in the house and couldn't get out of his front door as it was boarded up. We had to go down to reopen his door. When the inspector went into the flat the stench was really bad; they had to use breathing apparatus to enter. There were gangrenous bandages everywhere. The old man was put into hospital, where he eventually died. It was a sad tale of poor care by the council.

Then there was a tragic case of one of the lads on the depot, John Galloway, an electrician. He came to work one morning and complained about these large blotches on his legs. John was a very fit man, he was strong as an ox, but it developed into cancer. John had to be admitted into hospital, where part of his care was chemotherapy. The treatment was going O.K. for a couple of months, but then he was asked to have more chemotherapy. He refused to have any more, and he knew the consequences. John died shortly after; he was only 39 years of age. Most of the depot went to his funeral.

I remember one day I was looking out of the office window when I noticed the assistant storekeeper nosing around in the joiners' machine shop, so I told him to keep out of the joiners' shop. I went back into the office, two minutes later, this same person came dashing into the office holding his hand. He had been using the big table saw, and sliced off his index finger. I rushed him up to Whiston hospital, and he was off work for some time, but there would be no compensation pay as he had been warned of the danger.

The only good thing that came out of it was he kept his job, but he had ideas to put the onus onto Les Tasker, the shop joiner. I told him, "If you dare to blame Les, you will be out on your arse…quickly." Incidentally, Les Tasker was the brother of the famous Taskers do-it-yourself shop owner. His brother is a multi-millionaire. Les worked with his brother in a little shop in Westminster Road, Walton, which was where Taskers first started.

Working for the council, unlike working for most building firms, means you get a pension paid to you. I don't think the union ever fought hard enough for us, or really tried to get us a pension. The union employed rubbish solicitors, I found out after what happened to me at the Teaching Hospital and how my union solicitor handled my case. When I broke my ankle, I had a good case. Even the scaffolders admitted liability, but my union solicitor did nothing to help me. I called him a lousy swine, he actually told me to accept my wages for lost time. My case was an open and shut case.

I read a story about a man called Robert Noonan, whose pen name was Robert Tressall. He wrote "The Ragged Trousered Philanthropist", more commonly known as the Builder's Bible. This is a world famous book that was written in the early part of the 20th century, and should be read by every apprentice starting work. This book is the story of how men were treated by their so-called masters. It's a time we should never forget, because it's happening today, all over the world. Every man should be given a living wage.

Robert Tressall's grave was found in Walton Cemetery. Funds were found to clear the overgrown weeds, and a black gravestone was placed there. There was a dedication to the author, people like the M.P.s Eric Heffer, Eddy Lloydon and Bob Waring and several dignitaries from the unions were at the dedication, along with Robert Tressall's elderly niece.

CHAPTER THIRTY-THREE

The Political Landscape Changes

1979 was the year that the hated Thatcher Government took power, which ratcheted up the unemployment figures to three and a half million, and created a society for those that were well off. It was the Me Me society, with misery for the poor.

I don't think anyone will ever forget the miners' strike and the brutality meted out against the miners. Thatcher's aim was to break the miners' union, and then to curtail the power of all the other unions.

Who can ever forget the pernicious poll tax. A large mansion with two people living there, for example, would pay poll tax for just two, whereas six persons living in a council house had to pay three times the amount.

They first tried the poll tax in Scotland, then England got it.

The government saw the greatest demonstrations the country had ever seen, over a million strong. The police force was no match for them. The Tories soon dropped it. The poll tax only suited those who only thought for themselves, I had many an argument about it with some of my Tory friends.

Back then, "in the good old Tory days", old people would die of hypothermia because of lack of money for heating, unlike under the last Labour government where a grant of £250 was paid to each pensioner and there was a £400 heating allowance for each pensioner's household. There was also a further £70 in January to all pensioners over 60 years, and £400 to a pensioner at the age of eighty. I would say life is much better today, after Thatcher left power. She was kicked out of office by her own ministers. Then, under John Major's Conservative government, things improved slightly.

In 1997, Labour leader Tony Blair took power, with an overall majority of 179, the largest majority in history. The Labour party swept the board, employment got much better and inside of three years, 3 million people were back at work. Although Blair will unfortunately be remembered for Iraq, he did get rid of the tyrant and butcher Saddam Hussein. I think and hope that a future Iraq will someday have its own type of democracy. But it's got to be known, he will go down in history as the best Prime Minister we ever had. He also brought some sort of order to the area of the Balkans. But Iraq will forever be his nemesis.

When I lived in Edge Hill, I lived in the ward of Kensington. I was chairman of the ward. I was busy in many organizations, with my union, Trade Council, Chair of the Residents Council, and a member of the Family Social Action Group.

I took pleasure in taking this old, disabled chap to the swimming baths during the week. I picked him up at his house with my car. He was totally disabled. I had to take him to the swimming baths at Steble Street, I would have to undress him. Phew, did he pong, poor Peter… this was the only time he had a bath. I had to drive the car with the window open to get some fresh air. Some of the people in this group who came to the baths were totally blind, but we never refused anybody. The B.B.C. News of the North came to see what we were doing, they filmed it as a news item. Looking back, I don't know where I got the time. I still take an interest in my politics, but I don't go knocking on doors anymore, I just stuff envelopes for the M.P.

Eileen and I were invited to visit the Houses of Parliament by Maria Eagle. Although I have been many times before as a delegate, I never saw it in this light before. We had a meal there; the M.P.s certainly know how to look after themselves. We were very lucky to get tickets for the visitor's gallery, as tickets are hard to get hold of on Wednesdays, when it is Prime Minister's Questions in the chamber. We went up to the gallery and sat down, and after a while the Master at Arms asked us if we would like to sit in the cross gallery, where you can see both sides of the parliamentary debate.

There was a bloke sprawled across the seats, as if he owned the place. I recognized who it was - none other than Jeffrey Archer. I pretended not to know him, and I said, "Move up, mate." He was one of Maggie Thatcher's products, and the irony of Archer is, he cannot lose his title even though he served time in prison for perjury. You can lose a knighthood but not a peerage; what sort of a law is that?

It's a true fact that Mr MacMillan, during his period in office, had 27 relatives serving in parliament and nine relations in the cabinet.

These are the structures in Britain which I detest. I suppose this looks quaint to other countries like the U.S.A., but I certainly would like to change this system of peerages. Some of the House of Lords peers are from the bastard sons of yesteryear, people who treated the working class like shit beneath their feet. But the time is coming when the House of Lords hopefully, will be totally elected house. That's not to say that I don't favour a second chamber, I do want to see it happen and hopefully in my lifetime!

CHAPTER THIRTY-FOUR

My Children and Family Today

My children are all grown and employed now. Jacqueline, the eldest, is now the Head of the Audio Department in Whiston and St Helen's hospitals. She has worked for the N.H.S. for 24 years and has two children. Paul is a physicist, and looks after x-ray machines. He wears a lead lined jock strap. Samantha is nearly 16 years and Aidan is 13 years. Samantha won't let the grass grow under her feet and is very intelligent. Aidan is showing great promise and the teacher told his mum Aidan could take the class, his teacher is very proud of him.

Gerard is a civil engineer who has a degree in civil engineering and also a charted engineer's ticket. Gerard is married to Amanda (Mandy) and they have twin girls, who are nearly 15 years old now. The twins are not identical and they are both tall. Amy is so laid back she nearly falls over, whilst Rachael always likes to do every thing at speed and wants to join in everything. They both play the flute and are in the school orchestra, and Rachael also plays the tuba. I think they are university material.

Mandy, in her own right, has two University degrees. Intelligence normally is passed on to the children.

Gerard works out of an office in Cheshire and Mandy works as a sister in a hospice in Halton for Marie Curie.

They live in Helsby, Gerard worked for eight years in Abu Dhabi. He took his wife and their twins out with him. They had the good life out in Abu Dhabi, with very good schooling for the children. Eileen and I went out to visit them regularly for our holidays. We always went in January or February, because that's the coolest time, when the temperature only gets to the upper 70s.

The motorways in the Emirates are fantastic. They have four lanes on both sides and the run offs at the junctions are all stone finished, with palms and flowers mile after mile along the central reservation. These are watered with plastic pipes running underground, all the water is desalinated seawater.

Gerard took me to see one of his sites in the desert, a huge flyover. The concrete shuttering is much larger than what I was used to. One day, Gerard, Mandy, the twins, Eileen and I all piled into his 4x4 Nissan and we went out into the desert. There were also two other 4x4s, as Gerard's friends came along too. The rule is that you never go into the desert with one car, as it can be very dangerous if you break down. The greatest fun is riding over the huge sand hills. Gerard's car was the most powerful, he had a nylon tow rope and he was forever pulling the other two 4x4s out of the sand, including one top of the range Mercedes that always seemed to get stuck.

Another day, he took us to see the biggest lorry in the world. It was about 30 feet high; you could literally walk under it and each wheel had its own engine to move it.

We also went to the Corniche Promenade at Abu Dhabi where they had the highest flag pole in the world at 500 feet tall. It seems that the rulers in the Emirates have to have the biggest and best of whatever it is.

Then we went up to Dubai, which is a fascinating place, but full of bling bling. The Wild-Wadi is plenty of fun. I have never seen such a large water theme park. One pool is massive and they create huge waves, but there are plenty of lifeguards on hand. They have built a 7 star hotel, and in Dubai they have completed the highest hotel in the world at 2,400 foot tall, and they are well ahead in building the famous Palm Frond Island, the largest construction in the world. But I like Abu Dhabi better, not so artificial as Dubai.

My other son Paul works for Xerox in the printing industry, in the sales side. He works mostly in the southeast areas of the U.K. He has a good job, and has a company car and all the trimmings. Paul has two children - George is 12 years old and Lydia is 8 years old. George, I think, will be destined to be a palaeontologist when he grows up; he really knows a lot about ancient fossils, and he also loves looking at birds (the feathered type). Lydia will be an actress, as she is a drama queen. They live in Enfield. During the school holidays, Paul brings them up to see us. George is a very well mannered boy and a loving child. Lydia lets you know she's around, but she will do well in the world.

My daughter Michelle is employed with Sefton Council and works on the council finances. She has her own beautiful office. It is a job that carries much responsibility. Michelle is married to Colin Knox, who works in an office for a government-sponsored firm in insulation and heating. As I write this book, Colin has just been made redundant. I feel sorry for him, as unemployment is growing at an alarming rate.

I know she will not like me saying it, as Eileen is not getting any younger, but when all the family are here, she is the centre of attraction. She likes nothing better than to have all the grandchildren at our house, and she has a great relationship with Jacqueline and Michelle. Towards the end of every year, Eileen, Jacqueline, Michelle and Colin's mum Dot, go off to Lille for three days, and do a bit of shopping.

We always have a good New Year party at home. Most of Eileen's relations come, along with our gang and the children. We all gather outside to celebrate the New Year, sadly people do not venture outside their houses to celebrate anymore. We are the only house in the avenue that keeps up the tradition to use the front lawn; we join hands as the New Year is striking midnight and sing, "Auld Lang Syne".

One of the things I am very proud of is the fact that my

grandchildren are all excellent readers. They started reading from a very early age, which is important. Their parents take interest in their education, as all parents should do.

Eileen and I have lived in our present house for the past 32 years. Our house suites us fine, we don't need a mansion to be happy. I tend to be a Mr. Fix it, and love to potter around. My next door neighbour is George Grant Ross, as he likes you to emphasize Grant. He couldn't be anything else but a scotch. He is an 85 year old widower, who lost his wife Vera some years ago. He's a good neighbour, and I keep my eye out for him. I think that now I have finished with engines, after the work that has been done in this house over the years.

I need a rest. (I think!)

When Eileen reached her big 70th birthday, we had the best party ever. What a surprise she had in store. The children sent us both to the Empire Theatre, to a Saturday matinee, to get us out of the way. When we arrived home we were met by all the grandchildren at the gate of our house, balloons were tied everywhere. The biggest surprise was when we got in the house, all the catering was done, then we went round to the back of the house and we found that the whole garden was completely covered in marquees, they had heaters in them. The top decking, which is quite a large area, had the bar in a marquee. There were 70 people there including family and friends. Everyone said it was lovely party. We didn't get to bed till about 4am, but everybody seemed to enjoy themselves.

At the beginning of the year 2007, we went to Oman, on the holiday of a lifetime. The accommodation was 7 star and very expensive. We couldn't afford another holiday like Oman, much as we would like to, as it is all about cash.

I remember years ago in the old neighbourhood, parties were called "do's". Everybody was in the local pub, and when the pub had finished serving drinks at 10pm, the towel was put on the beer pumps, There was a shout from the barman "Time Please" hence 'the towel on'.

There were no off license shops or Tescos; you bought your beer in the pub and had to carry it home. This was known as 'jars out'. Sometimes the "do" would get out of hand, one word led to another and fists would be flying, but it always got sorted out somehow. There were those that would "Throw their hat in", in other words they were not invited to the party.

If you look back in recent history, from the middle part of the 19th century, the large brewers built pubs on nearly every street corner. In the earlier years, there were unlicensed premises. There were literally dozens of private houses that sold beer of their own making, I am talking about stills in the cellars, and this went on until they banned them towards the end of the 19th century. The outcome was public bars, hence the word 'pub',

In most pubs they had a tiny room called the snug, which was for women only. Women dared not enter the bar, which was the men's domain. If you saw a woman in a bar, you'd know she was a woman of the night (on the game).The posh room in the pub was known as the parlour, where there was a charge of 1p for service charge.

Public houses were built to appease the working classes; this was their only outlet to escape the misery of the environment they lived in. Women were treated like slaves, used as broodmares. It was common to see very large families of 10 children or more. Ignorance was rife and women didn't get full voting rights until 1928. I cringe to hear people talk of the good old days!

In Victorian times, poor people lived like dogs. The infant mortality rate was very high and people's lifespan was 40 years. This should have never happened, as this country was one of the richest countries in the world. In those days, Liverpool was a thriving city for the rich.

During the early to middle of the 19th century, the world's first Medical Officer of Health was introduced Dr Duncan. Hospitals were being built, but still the mortality was very high, mainly due to the living conditions of the poor, and poor food.

Seven year olds were working down in mines. Also children were put up chimneys to clear the soot. In these 'good old days' children even worked under spinning looms, a very dangerous place to be. The aristocracy didn't want to know, but thankfully the trade unions made the big changes to society.

I occasionally do like to visit London, both Eileen and I go frequently to visit our son Paul. I noticed a lot of street names in London that Liverpool has adopted, such as Hacken's Hay, Park Lane, Cheapside, Wapping, and many more.

If you look at the old White Star building at the corner of James Street and the Dock Road, you will notice the same architect built the Old Scotland Yard building in London. The same architectural lamps used in the Houses of Parliament are found in the Anglican Cathedral in Liverpool.

I found a relative whom I was not aware of when she placed a letter in the Echo. Her name is Sue Stamper. I contacted her. My wife and I went up to Skelmersdale to where she lived. Her father is my father's cousin, so that would make Sue my second cousin. I found that my youngest daughter Michelle is older than Sue. Sue had been tracing the family tree for some years, which is why she placed the letter in the paper.

The furthest she got back to was a John Stamper, dated 1750, he lived in Cumberland, and was a farmer. She also found that my grandfather's other aunt, whom I never knew, was called Adelaide.

I now have that family tree, which includes every grandparent from the year 1750.

I knew the aunt who lived in the front room of my grandparent's house was Aunt Hanna, my grandfather's aunt. To step into her room at Grandma's was like stepping back to the Victorian times, with white netted full curtains, the proverbial Aspidistra in the corner and a laced white antimacassar on her settee. She was a tiny lady, white hair with a bun, with steel-rimmed glasses and a long skirt. You had to be on your best behaviour; it felt like having an audience with the Queen Mum. She lived in my grandmother's housed until she died in 1936. Aunt Hanna was into her eighties, she would have been born in the 1850s.

I have a first cousin André living in West Suffolk, but I don't see her much of her. I suppose we are moving in different circles; she may contact me, sometime in the future!

Eileen and I went down last year to see André at her house in a tiny village, and she lived in a little chocolate box detached cottage, with a litch gate, with the preverbal Aga stove. André is the only first cousin I have, on my father's side of the family. She was born 17 years after me. I had not seen her in over 50 years, she's very nice.

At the weekends, the family all come to visit us. We always have a dinner, and after we have eaten we chat for a couple of hours at the table. The children eat in the utility room which is more comfortable for them, as they are at an age where they want their independence.

Eileen calls me Mr. Meldrew (I don't believe it!). Our house borders on the Mather Avenue Police Training College. Some time ago, they sent a notice to all the residents who lived on the periphery of the college about their plans to enlarge their car park. The plans indicated that the car park would finish one meter from my fence, it also meant the trees at the back of my fence would have to come down.

I said, "No way," so I, the sole objector, had to present myself to the planning department, along with the police representatives to argue my case. I won my case, and I also claimed £600 pounds, as during some work they broke part of my fence. This came about when the Police College decided to do some work at the back of my house and piled a load of earth onto the back of my fence. As I left the courtroom I looked at their representatives and said, "Not bad, played two and won two." I think old Mr. Meldrew was right, don't you?

The one good thing about having the Police College is that every time Liverpool or Everton win the F.A. Cup, or the League championship, the open-top bus starts directly at the back of our house. I remember one time Liverpool had won the cup, and before the entourage moved off I was talking to a friend of mine, Mike Black, who came over to see me as I stood on the back of my fence and happened to be the Lord Mayor of Liverpool. He was about to lead the cavalcade through the city. I said, after a while, "Mike, they're waiting for you." He said, "Let them wait!" as he was an Evertonian. It was funny to see Kenny Dalgleish shouting over at Mike, "We're ready, Mr. Mayor!"

I am looking forward to Colin's mum, Dot, having her 70th birthday soon. Coincidently, Dot went to Mount Carmel School, and she was in the same class as Eileen. Eileen is six months older. My daughter Michelle married Colin, they are very happy together.

My son-in-law, Paul Connolly, was recently showing me his father's seaman's discharge book. After glancing through it, I noticed he was the boatswain of a ship called the *Empire Endurance*, which was torpedoed in May 1941. This was a strange coincidence, as this was the same ship that George Gibbons, my mother's younger brother who was an O.S. (ordinary seaman), also sailed on at that time. Frank Connelly, my son-in-law's father, being the boatswain, would have been George's boss.

I didn't know this till years after Frank had died. I find this sad, because Frank would have said that he had known George, he could have related to me what had really happened that day. The story I had heard was that George was shouting for his mate, a man called Owen McCartney, a trimmer down in the stoke hold, who had been trapped down below with no chance of being saved as the torpedo had struck amidships. Apparently George was distraught, as they went to school together, and he was literally dragged into the very last lifeboat. George lasted 16 days, and then unfortunately succumbed, after becoming delirious from drinking sea water. The rest of the lifeboat crew was picked up three days later, on the 19th day. The sadness of all this is that George might have lived, had he lasted three more days, or got into his own lifeboat.

Frank had died some years before I saw his discharge book. Frank was not a man who, like many others, would not talk of the bad times; but it would have been interesting to talk to him about it.

The ship owners did not pay wages once the torpedo struck the ship, even if you managed to save yourself. By getting into the lifeboat, your wage contract would cease to operate. I explained this to Paul his son by showing him in the discharge book, where it shown the ship he had signed on. If the ship was lost there would be a line straight across the page, in other words, end of voyage. All that my grandmother received, when George was lost, was a small scrap of paper 6x4, with the words, "Sorry for the loss of your son" and signed George VI. These were printed in the thousands.

Earlier, before his fatal trip, George had had a small incident at home with his other brother, Harry. Due to this, he came to live with us at Brunswick Gardens in 1940. At this time, he had already done a few trips. However, my mother was worried in case something happened to him, so he returned home. A little later, in the early part of 1941, fate took a hand. He shipped out in the *Empire Endurance* and was torpedoed.

CHAPTER THIRTY-FIVE

Liverpool Then and Now

I am proud to be a native of Liverpool. 2008 was Liverpool's year of being European 'Capital of Culture'. Liverpool is the first English city ever to receive this award.

It was won by the nature of its people of Liverpool, not by the presentation of the city fathers - the citizens wanted it most. We were given the Charter Rights by King John in 1207 so recently celebrated our 800 year celebration. There were grand celebrations throughout the year. Billions of pounds have been spent on refurbishing the city and the centre of town has been transformed.

These transformations are going to mark the upturn of our city, a city with more beautiful listed buildings, than any other city outside of London.

It is the city where pop music was born, with the Beatles, the Merseybeats, Billy Fury and too many more to mention of the music industry, as well as top comedians and great actors. It is a city of wealthy benefactors; there are more parks than anywhere else in the country. It has two top football clubs. Liverpool was a city in which produced many inventors. We have the original School of Tropical Medicine, which has introduced programs for prevention of diseases such as malaria and sleeping sickness, and many other antidotes for tropical diseases.

One of the most beautiful buildings to see in Liverpool is the St George's Hall. It looks lovely when it's floodlit, and as Prince Charles had once said, it's the most beautiful building in Europe. This city could once again become the second city, as it was before.

When I was a child, all the buildings in Liverpool were one colour, black, because of the sooty atmosphere. During the industrial revolution coal was the first mineral fuel we used, the consequence to all that was having a dirty country. You have a look at the stone walls in and around the fields of Yorkshire, they are also black with soot, all the towns and cities of Britain were dirty.

But now, I think the last smog I remember was in 1963.

That year was also the coldest winter on record. I have heard it said that we must make the world a cleaner place and prevent more carbon entering the atmosphere, but maybe the damage was done during the whole of the 19th and the first part of the 20th centuries. However, of course we must still do something, to prevent further carbon emissions. "This for our children and grandchildren."

One of the things that make Liverpool a truly beautiful city is the parks. Liverpool's parks first came about mainly through the work of people like William Roscoe, and other benefactors, who had foresight and concern for the well-being of the citizens of Liverpool. He described parks as being the lungs of the city. He was one of the great visionaries of this city, he also had dreams of Liverpool becoming a second Florence.

It was a grand sight to see the Sefton Park lake, which had rowing boats and small motorboats for hire. People used to sail their model yachts on the lake. Near the rowing boat jetty, there was a fine model boat store. This building was a wooden structure with a beautiful design, but alas it was vandalized and burnt down. Recently the council have rebuilt a model building, plain but serviceable. During the wintertime, everybody went skating on the frozen lake. This was a fine sight to see, as lots of people skated across the ice. Sefton Park was noted for its large boating lake, but also for its beautiful Palm House and the Peter Pan statue, fashioned after Eros in London.

At that time, there were plenty of park keepers to keep

people under control. Nearby the café was an aviary, with some beautiful birds on show. There were lots of little streams, but the water was not stagnant, as it is now. Near to the aviary, in a small river, was the 'Jolly Roger', a scaled down model of the ship in 'Peter Pan'.

Between the large café and the boat lake, on a small island, was a bandstand. Bands would play there in the summer months. These were the civilized times of yesteryear. Sefton Park is still the largest public park in the northwest. I am glad to hear that the government is giving the council a grant to bring the park back to life. There are still beautiful Georgian and Victorian houses around the perimeter of the park. The Victorians also built the jockey sands, on which the toffs rode their horses.

In the 19th century Prince's Park, Calderstone Park, Greenbank Park and Wavertree Park were later added to Sefton Park. Calderstone Park has its beautiful show of flowers, Hydrangeas, Japanese gardens, a lake, and the famous "Calderstone Oak", said to be over 1000 years old. It also has the Calderstone sandstones. I believe the so called "Robin Hood's stone" in Booker Avenue was one of the original Calderstones. It may be possible it belonged to Josiah Booker, who had a farm in the vicinity. The score marks could have been caused by sharpening his scythes. Calderstone Park only became a public park at the turn of the 20th century. The property was owned by the McIver family, who was a partner of the famous Samuel Cunard shipping company. The name 'Calderstones' comes from finding Neolithic blocks of sandstone in the grounds.

Prince's Park has its own lake and has a gated small perimeter park, with some lovely blooms on show. Greenbank Park also has a lake, and a picturesque iron bridge. Wavertree Park has a huge field which is used for exhibitions, and nearby are the Botanical Gardens, which are currently being upgraded.

However, Roscoe probably never thought that the city would be so deeply over-populated. By the early part of the 19th century, things were really bad, so bad, that the working class lifespan was just forty years and the infant mortality rate was very high. We had serious over-population. Then there was the Irish famine, this didn't help things, in areas around the city centre people were living in appalling conditions.

They built the courts, which were so badly designed they were not fit for pigs to live in. Many families shared the same toilet, in some cases with just one water tap in the centre of the court. I don't know how the poor buggers lived in the wintertime when there was a freeze up. The houses were so close to each other there was not much daylight entering the court.

When I was a kid, there were plenty of cellar houses, sometimes called aer'ies. These had railings and a stairway down to the entrance of the basement, were families also lived, they never had much daylight coming into their windows.

Children would tie a skipping rope to the railings. Sometimes there might be grumpy old man living in the cellar, telling you to bugger off. Some of these types of houses also used the cellar for storing coal. There was a 15-inch round cast iron lid, for the coal man to deliver coal through. He'd lift the lid and the coal was thrown through the hole to the cellar below.

Today, as I stroll around the Pier Head, it saddens me to see the replacement of the world famous half mile long landing stage. I realize times change, and replacements have to be made, but the new stage is not as long as the old stage. The old stage was also twice the width of the new one, and it lasted 120 years.

I can still remember the little luggage ferries taking the horses and carts and steam wagons. This closed 1938. People would cross the river in the thousands. They would come down the floating roadway onto the stage. There were also four passenger ferry terminals, to New Brighton, Egremont, Wallasey and Birkenhead, and sometimes a ferry went to New Ferry, which is further up the river, past Cammell Laird's. There was always activity going on at the stage, as all the tram cars came to the Pier Head. It was the terminus for the trams, a hub of activity.

If you went to the Isle of Man, there were queues stretching from the head of the floating roadway, along to the end of Marine Parade, then down the gangway road to the stage. It was always interesting to watch the passengers who were coming off the transatlantic liners that were also berthed at the landing stage. There were sometimes two liners alongside. The passengers from the large liners crossed over to Prince's Parade to board a steam train at Riverside Station, to take them on to London. There are now huge modern buildings standing to where the station used to be. Those were happy days at the Pier Head.

I saw the naval supply ship *Bulwark* today; she looked a grand sight along the new landing stage. The Pier Head is still a very busy place today, as the new Museum of Life is taking shape and is to be opened in 2011, and there is also the extension of the Leeds to Liverpool Canal, extending from the Prince's Dock to the Canning Dock. The canal goes underground from the Prince's Dock and emerges from the tunnel opposite the Royal Liver Building, then goes in an open canal for about 300 yards opposite the Port of Liverpool Building. It finally goes into a tunnel and comes out into the Canning Dock. This was finished towards the end of 2009.

The Royal Liver clock face is the largest clock face in England, much larger than the clock face of Westminster clock. I hope they fix up the six-sided tower clock at the Clarence Dock, which is 180 years old. I am sorry to say they have removed the beautiful sandstone wall from the entrance to the car park at the Canning Dock. This is to make way for the new Forth Grace Building. It will be the best "Museum of Life" in the country.

While the excavation was going on for the Museum of Life they discovered the old Manchester Dock, which had been covered for more than a 100 years. They also discovered a part of the dock wall of the George's Dock, where now stands the mighty Liver Building, but was covered over for 150 years.

Before the war, there were many dairies dotted about Liverpool, some of which also had their own cows, with the shippery at the back. We had a dairy near our house that belonged to the Morgan's, he had a number of cows. When I was born, my mother couldn't ever give me enough milk. My mother always got our milk from the same cow; that dairy was in Threlfall Street. In my grandfather's day, it was owned in the 19th century by Tommy Handly's father, the well known comedian on the radio program called, "It's That Man Again" which was broadcasted during the war.

You often saw milk floats selling milk from the churn. The milkman had a gill or pint measure, which was poured into your jug. Sometimes we went to the dairy to get a penny's worth of butter milk. I remember a Miss Dwerryhouse in Robinson Street, who also had cows. She was a quite old, tall lady and a very staid woman; her little dairy was spotlessly clean. Nearby was Mae Ford's shop in Northumberland Street, a tiny grocer's shop that sold everything.

Opposite that was the paraffin oil shop. The sweets we'd buy here tasted of paraffin oil. Later on, it became a Greengrocers. The woman who owned it, Jean Cunningham, was a very good grafter and she made a good living. Most people used that shop; she always called you lad or girl, a typical scouser. At the corner of Beaufort street were two pubs, one was Mick Gilmartin's, and further up Northumberland street was I.I. Denny's the pawnshop. Next door was Jean Lockheart's, another greengrocer, Jean could work hard. At the corner of Robson street was a small sweetshop owned by a Mrs Ryan, there was Mr D Hendrick's coal yard between Mann Street and Star Street, and there was Mrs Lesball's tiny sweet shop who sold the first aerated lemonade - a large gas bottle was used to put the fizz into the lemonade into thick little six sided bottles. The price was 1p.

In Mann Street, there were old tenements that had a communal wash-house attached at the end of the building. At the turn of the century, this was quite an innovation. The women would light the fires under the boilers for the hot water. Opposite the tenements were the railway stables, which had 30 horses stabled there. We used to watch the carters taking the horses down Northumberland Street in the morning and bringing them back up again, after they had dropped off their carts at the huge Cheshire Lines warehouse on the Dock Road. As I mentioned earlier on, horses were a life-line in helping the war effort and the carters treated their horses with great respect.

What a sight to see the carter at lunchtime! He would put the shaft support under the shafts, to take the weight off the horse's shoulders, while he was having his dinner. The horse would get his feed bag put on before the carter would eat his lunch. The horse was fed on proven and always had a clean bucket, which the carter would fill up with water at the many stand pipes, but sometimes the public horse trough would be used. The last horse trough has been preserved. It is on the Dock Road at the bottom of Horsefall Street, near the Toxteth Dock.

The drinking fountains were very handy on a hot day. They were about three feet tall, cast iron, and had a dome head with a small iron pineapple on the top, a brass knob and a metal drinking cup, fastened with a chain. Nobody vandalized them at that time. At the bottom of the fountain was a moulded dish for the dogs to have a drink.

Another fine sight to see was the carts with huge loads going along the Dock Road. If the road was steep, the carts had to have a team of two horses to pull the loads. There were times when I saw two chain-horses pulling and one horse in the shafts. They would be thudding up Stanhope Street digging their hooves in the stone sets, trying to get a grip on the stone. Sometimes sparks would come off the horse's hooves, because most of the dock road was made up with granite sets. There would be quite a noise because the cart wheels were steel rimmed. You could not put a chain horse in the shafts, and you also cannot make a shaft horse do any chain work, due to their training.

There is a transformation happening in the City of Liverpool today, but there still is a lot to do in the housing situation. That is a problem that has been neglected by this excuse of a council. Things have got to change; this council has made enough crap decisions and we are now the worst performing council in the country. Millions have been thrown at it, but the council has made too many mistakes.

I remember years ago, it was privilege to serve on the council. Years ago we were lucky to get your tram fare. When I was a part of the old Borough Council, you never gave a thought to, "How much am I getting out of it?" There was no remuneration given to you, in fact the leader of the council, Hughie Dalton, had to use public transport at times.

These are our pride and joy.
Gerard 5 years, Paul 3 years, Michelle 15 months,
and Jacqueline aged 6 years

CHAPTER THIRTY-SIX

Finally Retirement...

Now I have retired, I have plenty to occupy my time with. I started building the porch and have just about finished the roof. And I even had time for a heart attack. I was rushed up to the cardiothoracic centre in Boardgreen Hospital and was operated on straight away, I was given an angioplasty. However, after 10 years, I am still a do-it-yourself addict.

I am a member of the "Harthill Bowling Club" of which I have been made Captain for this year 2010, of which I feel quite proud, as I have only been a member for four years. It is a very happy club, situated in Calderstones park.

I have seen and done many things in my life, and I have seen many changes during my lifetime. I wrote this book to tell people of my life story, and try to give a picture of the past. I hope you've enjoyed reading it. I urge everyone to remember all the events and changes in their own lives, and to write them down.

What I always say is that if you want to think old, you will be old. Age is in the mind - that is my philosophy. I am thankful for my children and my grandchildren. I have taken my grandchildren down to the Pier Head, and the Albert and Canning Dock areas. I'm hoping they will remember the area when they grow older, and the changes that took place in that area of the docks.

It wasn't the "Capital of Culture" that made me think about my love for Liverpool; I have always loved Liverpool. As Carl Jung described it, it is the "the pool of life".

Jack Stamper

To be a Miner

Who would get up and walk the streets at 5.30am?
A mad man?
No a miner.

Who would wear clothes many years old?
A tramp?
No a miner.

Who would walk in darkness not knowing where the passage ends?
A blind man?
No a miner.

Back aching work,
Dangerous work,
Who would be a miner?

Who would spend the day doubled over?
A hunchback?
No a miner.

Who would joke about falling stones?
A bad comedian?
No a miner.

Back aching work,
Dangerous work,
Who would be a miner?

Trolley past conveyer wheels turning, who would live like this?
A traffic warden?
No a miner.

Breathing bad air, swinging a heavy axe, only a miner would do that.

Bad aching work,
Dangerous work,
Who would be a miner?

Written by my daughter Jacqueline, aged 9 years